Archbishop John Carroll (1735-1815), founder of Georgetown University, as painted by Gilbert Stuart.

GEORGETOWN UNIVERSITY:

First in the Nation's Capital

Georgetown University:

FIRST IN THE NATION'S CAPITAL

Joseph T. Durkin, S.J.

FOREWORD BY ROBERT I. GANNON, S.J.

Garden City, New York
DOUBLEDAY & COMPANY, INC.
1964

CONTENTS

ILLUSTRATIONS

ILLUSTRATIONS

Hoya Saxal

The Hilltop, photographed by Mathew Brady

The Hilltop campus in 1889

[Between pages 54 and 55]

Marshal Foch at Old North

A perspective from the White-Gravenor terrace

The last cracking of the book before class

Herbert Hoover receiving an honorary degree

Alfred E. Smith at the 1941 commencement

Mask and Bauble promotes a play

Bob Hope speaking at a banquet

Eugenio Cardinal Pacelli receiving a degree

Pope Pius XII welcoming a Georgetown delegation

Field Mass at Fort Meade

Military Prize Competition Day

Healy's spires reflected in the Chesapeake and Ohio Canal

Father Edmund A. Walsh

President Dwight D. Eisenhower at the dedication of the Walsh Memorial Building

The stacks in the Riggs Memorial Library

Manuscript of The Adventures of Tom Sawyer

Baccalaureate Mass

Students receiving their degrees

ILLUSTRATIONS

ix

ILLUSTRATIONS

Pan American folklore fiesta

Miss Suzushi Hanayagi in Gaston Hall

Language students singing carols

Father Gerard J. Campbell presenting Anniversary Medal to Seán Lemass

Barbara Ward speaking at Georgetown

Gunnar Myrdal and Leon Keyserling listening to conference discussion

Dr. Alberto Lleras Camargo at a dramatic moment in history

Mass for President Kennedy at Old North

Chief Justice Earl Warren at the first convocation of the anniversary year

Vice-President Lyndon B. Johnson addressing the alumni banquet

Gabriel Marcel lecturing on "Science and Wisdom"

A session of a School of Foreign Service conference

Reporters gathering material on Poverty-in-Plenty conference

The Poverty-in-Plenty conference

Selassie I, Emperor of Ethiopia, receiving a degree

A student from Indo-China

Pablo Casals plays for the Glee Club

Professor Laurence Leite speaking on Baroque painting and sculpture

Father Edward B. Bunn, President, celebrating anniversary Mass

FOREWORD

Georgetown's whole story could never be told in such a modest little book. These few pages are intended merely to whet the appetites of still-promising alumni and stir the memories of old gaffers like me who are always ready to take off at the least suggestion for a trip to yesterday. Here we find more than suggestions. We can close our eyes and see again the "finest skyline in Washington," the Walks, the river and the grandstands; the faculty, the classrooms, Gaston Hall; the lighter spots in town, the food, the games, the bull sessions and the chapel; we can live again those four young years that passed like a breeze.

On reading this brief sketch, what occurred to me first of all was prompted no doubt by professional vanity. With so many celebrities sparkling in every paragraph, it seemed strange that so few presidents had made the grade. From Father Patrick Healy, who took over in 1873, to Father Bunn, now gloriously reigning—a matter of some ninety-one years—only Father Doonan, Father Nevils and Father Guthrie rate a mention of any kind. What stirred my emotions, however, was not vanity but the fact that I knew all but one of these illustrious fifteen.

The first three, of course, came into my life only after their terms were over. Father Healy and Father Doonan were in retirement at Georgetown during my college days and merely exchanged greetings on the campus. Father Richards, however, was my vacation superior at Keyser Island, good-as-gold but very precise. Although he told us that "the keynote of the villa should be hilarity" we were not expected to be frivolous. One evening when he heard me sing a parody on the Jesuit way of life, he let me know that my "comprehension of spiritual motives was distinctly inadequate." Father Whitney was president when my older brothers were in the Prep and I saw him only on days of major ceremony. Father Buel, on the other hand, was very close to the family. He was sued in the District Court by my father for expelling a brother of mine. Father Himmel, tall, bearded but handsome and friendly, was my first president in college; Father Donlon, my second and last. Father Creeden had been my prefect of studies for four years and got me out of Woodstock as a philosopher for the baccalaureate Mass. Father Lyons of Boston, I remember as an eloquent speaker with a terrifying laugh. Father Nevils, an old teacher of mine, built much of the New Georgetown and gave it additional tone. He was great on tone. He maintained that the oldest Catholic university in America had been founded not in 1789 but in 1634 when the Jesuits opened a school in St. Marys County "for the sons of the First Families of Maryland and—the better sort of Indians"! Father O'Leary had been a theologian when I was a philosopher, Father Gorman and Father Guthrie philosophers when I was a theologian, while Father Bunn succeeded me as a scholastic at Fordham in 1923, taking over my class, my corridor and my playshop. Of all the presidents then, in ninety-one years the only one I never had the honor of meeting was Father Daugherty, though of course we were all familiar with the Daugherty Memorial in the basement of the Old North. No wonder the text of this little book makes an old man glow.

Only one thing worried me as I read some of the more exciting passages. Was the class of 1913 worthy of its gallant forefathers? By the time we entered, a century had passed since the school catalogue demanded that new students be "literate 8 year olds of respectable behavior" and I am not sure now that we qualified on any of the three counts. Certainly we hadn't the spunk of those predecessors who could stage such a riot in 1833 that the chronicler wrote with some surprise, "not a Jesuit suffered the slightest wound." Seventy-five years later the best an effete generation could do, when refused a holiday in honor of St. Patrick, was to open all the windows when the tower clock struck nine and hurl pitchers and basins into the quad below. Perhaps the food had something to do with our decline. Back in 1813 the famous Father Peter Kenney could commend the president for having an Italian cook and for giving the boys toddy on feast days. (The bigger the boy, the stronger the toddy!) A century later when a meek senior complained about the tired ragout that was being served, the prefect of discipline was able to cow him by shouting, "Where's your school spirit?"

For alumni who studied medicine, law or foreign service, different phases of University life and different personalities will linger in memory, but all will read with pride the solid achievements of these 175 years. Some may express surprise at the rapid expansion since the war, the number of splendid buildings erected, and the millions in gifts and grants that have gone into all sorts of research. But the spiritual and cultural progress which impresses outsiders will be taken for granted by our own. These pages then, will make all of us just a little prouder to be Georgetown men —or (why not bring it up to date?) Georgetown women!

ROBERT I. GANNON, S.J.

ACKNOWLEDGMENTS

Georgetown University, in presenting this volume commemorative of its 175th anniversary year, wishes to thank Father Joseph T. Durkin, S.J., who furnished the text, Father Robert I. Gannon, S.J., who contributed its delightful foreword, Mr. T. O'Conor Sloane III, of Doubleday, who encouraged it, Professor Riley Hughes, who helped edit it and who gathered and selected the pictures which illustrate it, and the photographers, particularly Mr. Bob Young, Jr., University photographer, and Mr. Peter Carter, photographer for Anniversary House, both of whom captured Georgetown's many moods and faces.

In the writing of this brief account, many sources were consulted to support the historical facts. The author has drawn most heavily upon the following volumes of Georgetown history and has quoted from them: *Georgetown University: Origin and Early Years,* John M. Daley, S.J., Georgetown University Press, 1957, and *Georgetown University: The Middle Years: 1840–1900,* Joseph T. Durkin, Georgetown University Press, 1963. Both volumes contain full bibliographical references to the sources consulted in the present book, up to the year 1900.

Other sources, which the author gratefully acknowledges, are: *The Life and Times of John Carroll, Archbishop of*

Baltimore (*1735–1815*), 2 vols., Peter K. Guilday, The Encyclopedia Press, 1922; *John Carroll of Baltimore, Founder of the American Catholic Hierarchy*, Annabelle (McConnell) Melville, Charles Scribner's Sons, 1955; *The Jesuits and Education*, William McGucken, S.J., Bruce Publishing Co., 1932; *Georgetown College Journal*, various issues; *History of the Medical Society of the District of Columbia*, 2 vols., Medical Society of the District of Columbia, Washington, D.C.; *American Medical Research: Past and Present*, Richard H. Shryock, The Commonwealth Fund, 1947; the Georgetown University Archives; *The History of Providence Hospital*, Joseph Caulfield, M.D., Washington, D.C.; *Legal Education in the United States*, Albert J. Harno, Bancroft-Whitney Co., 1953; *The Georgetown Hoyas: The Story of a Rambunctious Football Team*, Columbia Publishing Co., 1947.

GEORGE H. DUNNE, S.J.
Director, 175th Anniversary Program

GEORGETOWN UNIVERSITY:

First in the Nation's Capital

JOHN CARROLL, PIONEER CHURCHMAN

The United States and Georgetown College were established in the same year, 1789, and were based on similar ideals. The one sought to protect man's freedom under law; the other, to show him how to use his freedom as a son of God for the highest individual and social ends. Both institutions, each in its own way, were implementations of the American Way of Life.

The creator of the College—John Carroll—was a typical product of the great age of the Founding Fathers. He was, like Washington, Jefferson, and Madison, a man of fundamental simplicity, clear thought, and serene courage. Like his eminent contemporaries, he had three profound loves—his God, his country, and his fellow man.

Born at Upper Marlboro, Maryland, in 1735, Carroll had received most of his early education at Saint Omer's College, in French Flanders. He had joined the Jesuit Order in 1753, had made his philosophical and theological studies at the University of Liège, in Belgium, and was ordained to the priesthood in England in 1769.

When, in 1784, the future founder of Georgetown became superior of the missions of the Catholic Church in the

United States and vicar apostolic or special representative of the Pope, he could claim acquaintance with many of the statesmen who were preparing the ground for the new republic of the Western world. He was a cousin of Charles Carroll of Carrollton, a signer of the Declaration of Independence. With Benjamin Franklin, John Marshall, Samuel Chase, and Charles Carroll he had undertaken, in the early years of the Revolution, an official journey to Canada in an effort to secure the support of the Canadians for the American cause. Later, he was more than once in the small group that rode to the outskirts of Baltimore to greet George Washington on the General's visits to that city.

In 1789 Carroll was appointed the first bishop of the American Catholic Church. Before the appointment was made, he had shown his appreciation of the need for accommodation to American ideas. He had warned the Roman authorities that his Protestant fellow citizens would dislike the appointment of a "foreigner" to the first Catholic American See. He therefore requested that the American Catholic clergy be permitted to nominate for the office three of their own number, the final choice to be made by the Pope. The plea was granted.

When Carroll assumed his new responsibility the total number of priests in the United States was about thirty. Carroll reported in 1790 that since his appointment as Prefect Apostolic he had "received or recognized" thirty Catholic clergymen who were then or had subsequently entered the country. Of these, most were "ex-Jesuits," a term that requires explanation.

The Society of Jesus had been canonically suppressed in 1773. Certain governments of Europe in the late eighteenth century were continually harassing the Pope in their efforts to receive decisive power over the Catholic Church in their territories. In this conflict the Jesuits vigorously supported the Holy See and consequently became *personae non gratae* to the political despots. The politicians sought, as part of their campaign against Rome, to weaken these allies of the Pope. By a series of decrees the governments "suppressed" the Order within their respective boundaries, and threatened the Pontiff with further annoyances unless he declared the Society of Jesus to be canonically nonexistent. This was not the first time the Holy See had been faced with the apparent necessity of sacrificing, at least temporarily, some members of the Church in order to protect the Church as a whole; and the Jesuits, according to their code of complete devotion to the Pontiff, were willing to be made expendable. Yielding reluctantly to pressure, Rome withdrew from the Order its canonical status.

So, at the time of the founding of Georgetown, the former members of the Order in America were "diocesan" priests, that is, priests attached to the ecclesiastical jurisdiction of Baltimore, with Archbishop Carroll as their superior. (Carroll himself, because of his new office, would have been obliged by Church law to resign from the Society even though the organization had been legally alive. The duties of a bishop preclude being bound by the three vows that constitute the status of a member of a religious Order.) In 1789 the Baltimore diocese embraced the whole of the United States.

The "ex-Jesuits" regarded themselves as belonging in spirit to the Society of Jesus, and they looked forward ardently to a restoration of the Order. (This was to occur in 1814.) In their devotion to their "spiritual mother," no one was more enthusiastic than Carroll.

That these priests should conceive the idea of establishing a school is not surprising. The Jesuits had planted liberal arts colleges and professional schools throughout Europe since the late sixteenth century. Their prestige as educators was high, and their services in the field were widely sought. Their teaching methods combined the ideals of Christian Humanism with the values of Renaissance learning.

The initial prospectus for Georgetown College was written by Carroll in 1786:

The object of the proposed Institution is to unite the means of communicating Science with an effectual Provision for guarding and preserving the Morals of Youth. . . . It [the Establishment] will therefore receive Pupils as soon as they have learned the first Elements of Letters, and will conduct them through the several Branches of Classical Learning to that State of Education from which they may proceed with Advantage to the Study of the higher Sciences in the University of this or those of the neighboring States. . . . Agreeably to the liberal Principle of

4

our Constitution, the Seminary will be open to Students of every Religious Profession. They, who, in this Respect, differ from the Superintendent of the Academy, will be at Liberty to frequent the places of Worship and Instruction appointed by their Parents; but with Respect to their moral Conduct, all must be subject to general and uniform Discipline.

Funds for the project came from two main sources: the Catholic clergy and a few wealthy Catholics in England. A site for the school was purchased "at George Town on the Potowmack," and in the early spring of 1788 Carroll reported:

We shall begin the building of our Academy this summer. In the beginning we shall confine our plan to a house of sixty-three or sixty-four feet by fifty, on one of the most lovely situations that imagination can frame. It will be three stories high. . . . On this Academy is built all my hopes of permanency and success of our H. Religion in the United States.

A possible anticipation of modern methods of protecting the laboring man is suggested by a stipulation made by the subcontractor:

. . . the said Henry Carlile [is] not to be obliged to be at the charge of glazing nor of doing anything on the inside of the said house except the laying of the joysts. The said Henry Carlile having agreed . . . only for the erecting the Hull or Carcase of the said House.

GETTING UNDER WAY

Since a college must have a president, Carroll set out to find one. His standards were high, and manifested his bias toward American ways. The head of the school, he insisted, must be

capable of abstracting his mind from the methods used in the [European] colleges where he has lived, so as to adopt only as much of them as is suited to the circumstances of this Country, and of substituting such others as are better adapted to the views and inclinations of those with whom he has to deal.

The College received its first student on November 22, 1791. He was William Gaston, of North Carolina, who would later represent his State in the United States Congress. Father Robert Plunkett, one of the "ex-Jesuits," had been appointed the school's first head. Besides two seminarians, John de Mondesir and Samuel Brown, and Father Francis Neale, there were only three other members of the faculty. (Until 1868 Georgetown, besides being a school for young lay students, would also be an institute for the training of candidates for the Jesuit Order in liberal arts, philosophy, and theology.)

There were three divisions of the "lay" school—elementary, preparatory, and college. The first of these was what we today would call a grade school; the second a high school; the third (not opened at first for want of suitably prepared students) corresponded to our liberal arts colleges. At this time and for many years afterward Georgetown's lowest division was open to any literate eight-year-old of respectable behavior.

By the close of 1793 there were sixty students in the three divisions. Two years later another building—Old North—had been constructed and put to use. The addition of three new teachers in 1793 had increased the size of the faculty to seven. The tuition charge, £10 (about $44.40) per year, was paid half-yearly in advance. Board on the same terms was £30 (about $133.20) per annum.

WHAT THEY STUDIED

The curriculum was modeled on that of the typical "Classical Academy" of the period. In the elementary classes the boys studied reading, writing, English grammar, arithmetic, geography, "beginner's" Latin, and sometimes the foundations of Greek and French. Most of these basic courses were expanded and deepened in the "preparatory" division, with the addition of some new subjects, particularly in the natural sciences. On the highest, or "college," level the concentration was on literature (Latin, Greek, and English), natural science, and philosophy.

What strikes the observer today is the unusually large number of authors sampled, within the range of the Latin and Greek Classics. If a boy began in the lowest class at George-

7

town and survived to the end of the College course, these are some of the writers he had studied: Cornelius Nepos, Sallust, Livy, Cicero, Ovid, Lucian, Xenophon, Vergil, Horace, Homer, Caesar, Theocritus, Thucydides, Quintilian, Demosthenes, Juvenal, Persius, Sophocles. In English literature, the emphasis was on the neoclassic prose masters and poets of the eighteenth century and the current masterpieces as the Age of the Romantics unfolded.

Another noteworthy feature of the Georgetown system of studies was, at all stages of the student's training, a heavy stress on English composition. More time was devoted to practice in writing English than to similar exercises in Latin and Greek, for the Jesuits believed that knowledge should be not only a possession but a tool; it should be translatable into the fitting word. Hence, exercises in oral argument and declamation were encouraged by various devices, particularly the debating societies. The Georgetown student was ready at almost all times to make a speech, especially if there was somebody around to contradict him.

The curriculum awarded considerable time to the study of the French language. This subject was introduced in the lowest classes and continued during several years. It was referred to by a later official of the College as "the beautiful language . . . without a knowledge of which a person cannot be truly civilized."

Georgetown, from her earliest days, gave ample room to the study of the natural sciences. In 1818 there were courses in chemistry, physics, and astronomy. At many of the "public exhibitions" and commencements, students performed experiments in chemistry. At the December examination of 1821, the boys were asked to "explain and demonstrate" fifty propositions from physics. A visitor to the College in 1833 beheld in the museum "the largest electrical machine" he had ever seen. In the College Library at the midpoint of the century the natural science section was numerically the largest.

The Georgetown teaching method at this time was based on the optimistic theory that if constant dropping of water would wear away a stone, constant repetition of lessons would educate a boy. The instruction was intense rather than broad. Five lines of Greek or Latin thoroughly assimilated were regarded as more valuable than wide reading less thoroughly grasped. (This was the method used by Hadley, the great classicist at Yale.)

For the Georgetown student, the academic life was a succession of "oral repetitions," "memorizing," and examinations. The postulate was that the entrance of knowledge would not be so bloody if made over and over again. Nothing was taken for granted by the teachers save the natural tendency of youth to forget.

DISCIPLINE

For administering these courses of study and for maintaining order in the school, some rather patriarchal rules, customary in the small academies of the period, were laid down. On the president was placed a large share of the burden of executing the regulations. He was to take part in all the major examinations of the students himself. He was to visit the classes frequently. The grim power of making "general regulations concerning the degrees of punishment to be inflicted" also belonged to him.

Somewhat later the students were obliged to wear a distinctive uniform whenever they appeared off the campus. One version of this was a "blue coat, blue pants, and red waistcoat with large yellow buttons." Strictly forbidden was "the frequenting of disorderly company or houses; going to publick houses or gaming tables"; nor must the students "go beyond the limits assigned them, play at games of hazard or drink intemperately."

On the point of discipline, Carroll was inclined to be liberal rather than strict. He said, some years after the founding of the College, that certain of the rules imposed on the students were "too monastic" and "not calculated for the meridian of America." The boys were being denied "that liberty which all here lay claim to," and he laid down the following commonsense general principles:

Indeed it is a difficult problem to solve, what degree of liberty should be allowed in literary establishments [the contemporary name for a liberal arts college], and never have I been able to satisfy my own mind on this subject, though it has been much employed in thinking of it. Theory and experience are constantly at variance in this case; for though the principles of religion and morality command, or seem to command, the instructors of youth to restrain their pupils from almost every communication with the men and things of the world, yet that very restraint operates against the effects intended by it, and it is too often found that on being delivered from it, young men, as when the pin that confines a spring is loosened, burst out of confinement into licentiousness, and give way to errors and vices, which with more acquaintance with the manners and language of the world, they would have avoided.

It was not Carroll's intention, of course, to eliminate all punishments, and his attitude was piously imitated by the College administrators.

A typical penalty consisted in a boy being "sent to the clock." The culprit would stand for a specified period beside the ancient timepiece at the turn of the stairway leading to the president's room in Old North. Aggravating the penalty if not the crime was the fact that the malefactor, while standing there, must study "those books . . . so much hated and neglected," as the prefect of studies phrased it.

Corporal punishment was employed at times. The robustness of a past generation is suggested by the attitude of the priest who wrote to his younger brother, then a student at Georgetown: "The more they whip you, the better I will like them, at least until you can show me a good premium [prize for studies], honorably acquired." This earnest cleric, after praising on Scriptural grounds the use of the rod, recommended to his correspondent that the latter should even "go . . . occasionally to [the] Master with that vivifying instrument in . . . hand and politely request him as a particular favour to administer . . . some of its rare and surprising qualities."

DAILY ROUTINE

The boys rose in summer at 5:00 A.M. and in winter at 5:30. "No one," the later Rule Book rather unnecessarily prescribed, "shall rise before the appointed time, without express leave from the Prefect." First on the schedule was a run out to the yard pump for "washing and combing." (In this era young gentlemen wore their locks long.)

At 5:45 came morning prayers, then Mass at 6:00. Breakfast was still an hour and three-quarters away, the time after Mass being devoted to study until 7:45. Classes began at 8:15 and continued until 11:15, when the students walked in silence, single file according to height, to dinner.

Dinner was followed by "recreation" or playtime for an hour and a half. Spacious playing fields were available. The popular sports were handball, a rudimentary kind of football that was probably more like present-day soccer, and gymnastic exercises. Fencing and boxing also had their devotees. Baseball would not come into vogue until after the Civil War. That a sense of irony was not lacking in the Jesuit author of the Rule Book is hinted by the admonition that during time of recreation the study hall was locked and no one was allowed to have a book.

Afternoon classes were held from 2:15 to 4:45, followed by a half hour's recreation. Another study period began at 5:30, with supper at 7:00. After night prayers, bedtime was 8:30.

Long walks in groups accompanied by a Jesuit "prefect" were enjoyed on holidays. The excursions were not always dull. In 1824, on one of their marches, the Georgetown boys staged a pitched battle with some Columbian College students who had captured a Georgetown banner. To "legalize" the attack by the Georgetown boys, the latter, says an old diary, "were led by their prefect."

Also popular on holidays were boat trips down the Potomac. A favorite stopping place was Mount Vernon, where, on a later occasion, the students were "kindly received by Col. Washington [the General's nephew, Bushrod]."

An authority on Georgetown's early history expresses surprise that the boys were sometimes allowed to go "to the races," but it might seem they were safe enough there, since the maximum amount of spending money allowed was twelve and a half cents a week.

There were, of course, occasional bolder spirits who pressed their luck too far. The following sad story was written by a student about two of his classmates:

I am about to inform you [he is writing to his father] of a little circumstance which has taken place here. . . . [X] and [Y] have been expelled . . . on account of their bad conduct. Mac did not expect they would expell him for he was often heard to say, that they loved money too dearly. . . . [The party went] with the Prefect to Congress. . . . When opposite one of the principal hotels in Washington City they met a young lad who invited them to take a glass of good old apple jack. . . . In this many hours rolled away, nay, even days, and neither James or Mac returned to College.

An almost constant preoccupation of the Georgetown students was food. By and large, their anticipations were not disappointed. One of the firm policies of the College board of directors was that no program of economy should be applied to the detriment of the boys' menus. In a directors' meeting it was resolved that the students' provender should be "clean, copious, and good." That this resolve was implemented is evident from such facts as the following passage in Father John M. Daley's *History* of the College:

The Lenten season, always a poser for any cook, opened in 1813 with the typical Lenten fare of the period: "Codfish and potatoes, parsnips (fried), and eggs. Rice with milk, somedays; other days apple pyes." The menus on festival days were of course more elaborate: "on Christmas day (most of the boys spent this holiday at the College) the Students had for dinner: first dish, Corn'd pork and Cabbage; 2nd (dish), Smoaked Beef and Turnips; 3rd, Spare Ribs Roasted and 4th Roast Geese, Toddy, Apples, Cakes and Crackers." The mysterious note in the Christmas menu is wrapped within an enigma by a recurring notation: "The students had nothing extraordinary for dinner except Toddy."

On one special occasion, "after breakfast egg nog [was served] to [the] students seated at their tables, according to the distribution of large and small, that of the large boys being something stronger."

THE EARLY LOOK

Exteriorly the College, at the turn of the nineteenth century, had the air of a Southern plantation, with two rambling country schoolhouses facing each other on a low plateau at one end of the property. Old South was a Colonial structure of decent competence but somewhat apologetic mien; Old North, at that time the "new" building, was large, awkward, and severe-looking. Sweeping away on all sides from the buildings was the most attractive part of the College estate —almost 150 acres of rich Maryland truck-farm land. The wide-spreading girdle of meadows, orchard, and woodland sealed the College off from the environing civilization and provided the illusion of a cultivated wilderness existing all to itself. Georgetown was nothing if not solitary.

Everything inside the buildings was on a small scale— classrooms, dormitories, dining hall, and "auditorium," and the short (often dark) corridors and narrow stairways. Walls and ceilings were for the most part unadorned, with an unfinished appearance; rooms looked like reformed barracks. "Tired Colonial" was the style attributed to these interiors by a visiting wit.

Georgetown at this time was a snug little school of seventy-six students, some two-thirds of them being boarders. Of the total number, a little more than three-fourths were boys of grade-school or junior high school age, enrolled in the "preparatory" department. Attending the senior class of the College division were also a few Jesuit seminarians.

AN EMINENT VISITOR

On a day in early August 1797 a horseman rode up to the College gate and hitched his steed to a post. He wished to visit his two young nephews, Bushrod and Augustine, who were students at Georgetown. He was at once recognized and excitedly prepared for; he was George Washington, recently retired from the Presidency.

A reception was tendered him by the faculty, probably in the Old North parlor; the students were assembled either in the study hall or on the lawn between the two buildings, and an address of welcome was read to him by student Robert Walsh, later to become one of America's distinguished journalists. If, as alleged, the speech was hurriedly composed for Master Walsh by a faculty member, it was probably delivered with no less fervor for all that.

Archbishop Carroll was not present to greet his old friend. If he had been there, he would have been delighted to display his academy to the general, and would have regarded the visit as a special blessing conferred on the school. Shortly afterward the president of Georgetown, Father Guillaume Dubourg, was invited by Washington to dine at Mount Vernon.

THE GREAT GRASSI

Three men practically carried Georgetown College on their
backs during the first three decades of the nineteenth century. They were Fathers John Anthony Grassi, Peter Kenney, and Thomas Mulledy. By being consistently critical of
her condition, they saved Georgetown. They were stern and
demanding foster parents to John Carroll's fledgling.

All had not been going well when Father Grassi became
president of the College on August 11, 1812. Six years before, Archbishop Carroll had actually recommended the
temporary suspension of the school. Student registration
had fallen off sharply; in the autumn of 1806 there were
only thirty-four boys on the rolls. "We cannot expect," the
archbishop had warned, "parents to send their children to
lodge and study in unplastered and cold apartments"—a
reference to the still-unfinished state of the Old North
building. He urged that a breathing space be taken by sending the boys away for a year or two until the College could
provide ampler accommodations and a more competent faculty. This proposal was not carried through, but it was in-
dicative of the seriousness of the situation.

Soon after Father Grassi's accession to the presidency the
question arose again of moving the College—students and
equipment alike—to New York City. The argument was that

the city of Washington was a backwoods town with no future, an unsuitable location for a school. New York, on the contrary, was rapidly becoming the metropolis of the nation. Once transferred to that promising site (so the argument ran), Georgetown College would blossom like a rose. The proposal was backed by Father Anthony Kohlmann and several other influential American Jesuits.

Father Grassi at once took two vigorous steps. With the support of Archbishop Carroll (who had changed his mind about the College since 1806), he scotched the idea of moving to New York. He predicted that Washington would one day be a world capital and declared that no city in the nation would then be more suitable for the home of a great university.

More important, he re-energized the faculty, strengthened the curriculum, and repaired and enlarged the physical plant. He insisted that the College be self-critical, that it face its deficiencies frankly and correct them. The great danger, he warned, was complacency.

Father Grassi was of medium height, with short-cropped hair, rather quizzical auburn eyebrows, sharp hazel eyes, and a firm chin. His complexion was ruddy and his voice was gentle. He was incisive in his movements.

He was born at Bergamo, Italy, in 1775. While still in his twenties he had been rector of the College of Nobles at Polocz in Russia. He had then, with two Jesuit companions, made a trip by dog sled in midwinter over the Russian plains to Sweden, as the first stage of an anticipated missionary expedition to the court of China. The emperor of that country was seeking instructors in the natural sciences, and the Jesuits had been picked to fill the need. But the project collapsed, Father Grassi being finally shunted to the Jesuit college at Stonyhurst, England, where he studied the teaching methods. In 1810 he was sent across the sea to Georgetown College.

Insatiably inquisitive, he was avidly interested in the people around him, in natural science, and in the technique of administration. He wrote a perceptive essay on the habits of the people of the United States. Constantly trying to discover what made the Americans different from Europeans, he usually gave the Americans the better of the comparison.

At Georgetown he constructed, with the aid of another Jesuit, wooden models of the Copernican system, devised a terrestrial globe, calculated eclipses, and determined the altitude of the sun.

He was fascinated by the art of governing an educational institution. If other presidents of Georgetown regarded their office as a sobering responsibility, Father Grassi looked on it almost gaily, as an opportunity for solving new puzzles and for learning more about how to manage boys and men wisely. He administered the College with the Italian touch of easy grace and hard realism.

BURNING OF THE CAPITAL

In August 1812, British troops invaded Washington and burned the Capitol, the White House, and other government buildings. Father McElroy, then stationed at Georgetown, reported later that the flames "were so great that a person could read at the College [by their light]." The citizens of the city of Georgetown were badly frightened by what they feared would be the next eventuality—a British attack on that ancient borough. Some of the braver inhabitants, it was said, began to construct barricades in the streets. But the crisis soon passed and Georgetown was spared an invasion.

A letter opened by Father Grassi on December 9, 1814, reported an event of great relevance to the College. The communication, from Archbishop Carroll, announced that the Society of Jesus was formally restored throughout the world. This re-establishment of the corporate life of the Jesuits could not fail to be an added stimulus to the Order's loyal members at Georgetown.

In the fall of 1817, seven or eight Indian chiefs, in Washington to confer with President Monroe regarding land matters, visited the College. They expressed their thanks for the ministrations of the Jesuit missionaries in Indian territories, inspected the school, and enjoyed a good dinner with the faculty.

NEW IMPETUS FROM ROME

Father Grassi's presidency ended in the summer of 1817 and he returned to Rome. His absence was felt almost immediately. The College, deprived of his firm hand, showed signs again of withering on the vine. The "close Georgetown" party once more raised its voice. "It might be expedient," wrote a spokesman for this group, "to shut up the college for a certain number of years say three or four or five years."

In the midst of mounting discouragement Father Peter Kenney arrived in 1819 from Rome as a special visitor, sent by the Jesuit Father General to survey the general situation of the Society in the United States. Dissatisfied with the academic quality of the College faculty, he decided that some of the younger teachers should be sent to Europe for further intellectual training, and in the early summer of 1820 six Jesuit seminarians embarked for Rome. Three of them would later become presidents of Georgetown, and one an important prefect of studies at the College. Another would fill the office of provincial of the Maryland-New York Province of the Order. The infusion of the superior educational methods of the Continent through the instrumentality of these European-trained Jesuits was to result in better teaching and a more vigorous intellectual atmosphere in future years.

Father Kenney, a level-headed native-born Irishman, was prudent, considerate, and broadminded. His attitude toward America was manifested in his retort to a European fellow priest who had expressed a fear that the young American Jesuits studying at Rome would retain their "republican" views. "If they are to have any opinion in politics," wrote Father Kenney, "why should it not be in favor of their native government? Those who fled from absolute tyranny in Europe should be the last to complain of the spirit of a government which gives fair and equal advantage to the Catholic Religion."

LAFAYETTE AT OLD NORTH

In the midst of one of the College's less successful periods, the Marquis de Lafayette, hero of the American Revolution, visited the campus. A troop of light cavalry escorted him to the College gate, he was entertained in the Old North parlor, and he apparently enjoyed himself much more than did his hosts. The Marquis had embarrassed Catholics during his American tour by what seemed to them a slighting of the Catholic religion to which he had been born. He had refused, according to report, to kneel during Mass at the Baltimore Cathedral, and had provoked the aged Charles Carroll of Carrollton to whisper angrily, "Either kneel or sit down." In Boston, when invited to attend Mass, he had (so it was said) replied that he was going to worship at a

Presbyterian Church. Four days before coming to Georgetown he had accepted the highest honors of the Order of
Masons. His apparent inclination to play the field might
have been responsible for the "frightfully bungling speech"
of welcome made to him by the Jesuit superior at Georgetown.

THE MULLEDY ERA

The presidency of Father Thomas Mulledy, from September 1829 to December 1837, witnessed the real upsurge of
the College. Described as "a genial, rough-and-ready, independent American," Father Mulledy—a native of West Virginia and a "man's man"—on one occasion took off his cas-
sock and physically subdued an unruly student. He must
have been marked by more valuable qualities than mere
physical strength, however, for he was three times recommended for American bishoprics, one of them being that of
New York. He exemplified in his person and intellectual
equipment the fine flowering of Father Kenney's project of
1820—the producing of an American scholar by contact with
the best in the European university tradition.

Under Father Mulledy the course of studies was reorganized, the faculty improved in quality, and a systematic
campaign undertaken to advertise the school more widely.
More rigorous academic standards were introduced. The
students were obliged to do weekly compositions in English,

weekly translations from Latin or Greek into English, and written exercises daily in Latin, Greek, and French. An hour and a quarter each day was devoted to mathematics, and a total of five hours of study was demanded as a preparation for classwork. The rejection of several students for graduation was a sign that the Georgetown bachelor's degree was a prize that had to be worked for. Every effort was made to keep the classes small so that the boys could receive individual attention.

THE PHILODEMIC SOCIETY

One of the signs of increased academic health was the establishment of the Philodemic Debating Society by Father James Ryder. This most famous of the student associations of the College was founded in 1830 to assist in the cultivation of the arts of argument and oratory—and another virtue described by one of the student officials of the organization:

. . . We endeavored to adapt the Philodemic Society to the peculiar institutions of our country; we went back to the source of all power—to the foundation stone of the republic—the people. As our government is an anomaly in governments . . . so must necessarily be every institution (like the Philodemic) which has the same foundation, and has for its object the support of that system which grows out of it.

Therefore did we base our infant society upon the same permanent pedestal, by which the stupendous fabric of our government is supported—the people. The object of thus establishing it on an attachment for the people, was a wish at some future time to assist our country-men in watching over and defending the government which guaranteed to all the inestimable blessing of liberty. In cherishing a love for, and identifying ourselves with, the primitive elements of our government, we necessarily blended all our feelings in the government itself.

THE COLLEGE AND THE FLAG

The patriotic aim of the debating society reflected one of the basic purposes of the school as a whole. The insistence of American Jesuit educators on love of country is one of the distinctive facts of the history of Catholic education in the United States. An observer of the 1830s wrote this about the College:

The character of their national celebrations, the institute of their Philodemic society, the spirit breathed through the speeches at their commencements, attest their patriotism, and ardent devotion to our national institutions, and the care that is taken to implant in the youthful breast a lofty love of independence, and a generous patriotism. Perhaps there is not in the country an institution where a greater portion of republican feeling can be discovered, whenever occasion calls it forth. . . . Their essays, their speeches, their poetry, are pregnant with the *vis divina,* that fire of freedom, and that *dulcis amor patriae* which would do honor to the youths of Rome and Athens in their most flourishing days.

EXPANSION

When Father Kenney returned to the College for another tour of inspection in 1830, he found little to change. Father Mulledy's revival of the school was well under way. The practical mind of the Visitor was shown by his approval of the new culinary situation: "I am quite pleased that you got an Italian cook. . . . If the smoke be kept out of the Kitchen Father Ryder (in charge of these matters) will have every help to make the refectory rival the best that can be found in Italy."

Soon after he became president, Father Mulledy undertook to provide more classroom and dormitory space. A new structure was ready for occupancy in June 1833, after the minor miracle of financing that was almost always to accompany any physical expansion at Georgetown. The building, given the name of the president of the College, was more than ninety feet long and had "noble cellars on the basement, a refectory on the second, a study in the Third, and a chapel with covered ceiling on the fourth story."

IMPORTANT GIFTS

Gifts from three quite different sources helped Father Mulledy in his efforts to develop the school. In March 1833 President Andrew Jackson signed an Act of Congress conferring on

Georgetown College $25,000 in District of Columbia lots.
(A simultaneous and equal gift was made to Columbian
College.) In an action scarcely applauded at Georgetown,
Senator William King, of Alabama, voted against the bill,
although he had two young relatives pursuing their studies
at Georgetown.

The second and more important benefit came in the same
month from the Holy See: a charter granting Georgetown
the status of a Pontifical University. By this grant from the
Pope, Georgetown was empowered to confer on qualified
scholars the highest degrees in theology and canon law.
The University still possesses this right but in recent years
has not exercised it.

More complicated was a gift of $7000 made to the College
in 1834 by the widow of Admiral Stephen Decatur. The
sum was said to be the officer's prize money from the
Tripolitan war. A string attached to the donation was Mrs.
Decatur's request that the College should pay her an an-
nuity, while she lived, of $630. The College accepted this
condition, and Mrs. Decatur proceeded to live on until 1860,
by which time the annuities paid were more than twice
the amount of the lady's gift to the Jesuits. The College
was satisfied, however, since the $7000 had been badly
needed in 1834.

REBELLION

In November 1833 occurred one of the student "rebellions" that have periodically illuminated the pages of Georgetown's history. The importance of this particular outbreak has been exaggerated; better executed revolts would follow —notably in 1850—and a similar affair of the late 1850s would display far more imagination and verve. The trouble was precipitated by the expulsion of a student who, on a walking excursion, had visited several taverns. His classmates rose in indignation at the penalty meted out, and violence was manifested by both sides. At the climax of the rebellion a group of angry students attempting to "rush" the prefect in the study hall was repulsed by a solid phalanx of Jesuit Brothers. The administration finally won. Forty boys were expelled, and ten more "resigned." The College diarist noted that "amid all these dangers none of the [Jesuit] Community suffered the slightest wound."

During the latter half of the 1830s the school had about one hundred and fifty students; about one hundred of them were boarders. It was a well-managed school of the traditional type, cozy, conservative, and, although always open to students of other religions, Catholic. It was content to do a limited but important job well, the imparting of a sound general and Christian education to a select group of boys. While the students led a rather cloistered existence on their solitary hilltop, they were given a few opportunities to observe the outside world. Occasionally a group would visit the Capitol, to listen to the historic debates of Webster, Clay, and Calhoun. And the resplendent College Cadets serenaded the White House almost annually and were warmly welcomed by the President. It was customary, moreover, for distinguished men to visit the College to deliver addresses—often with frankly political motives.

The natty uniforms and neat marching steps of the College Cadets symbolized, in a way, the state of the College as well as that of the Union. Indeed, the future of the College seemed, at this time, the more secure of the two. Northern and Southern congressmen were coming to blows on the floor of the House as the slavery debate progressed, and in 1838 and 1839 the sections of the nation were scarcely as united as the tight little ranks of the Georgetown College students from both sides of the Mason-Dixon line.

GREAT TEACHERS

Among the outstanding faculty members during the forties were the three Jesuits John Prendergast, Daniel Lynch, and Joseph O'Callaghan.

Father Prendergast was, according to report, "a large rawboned man, of strong Celtic characteristics and thoroughgoing methods. . . . He was the best weight-thrower or shot-putter in the house." In the classroom he was a ruthless perfectionist. He could squeeze an amazing amount of meaning out of a Latin or Greek word. Greek prepositions were like putty in his hands. He made almost a religion out of exactness.

Father Lynch, a native Irishman, was at first professor of rhetoric, Greek, and history at the College, and from 1851 to 1858 vice-president and prefect of studies. He was a remarkable linguist and philologist, with a knowledge of Hebrew, German, Spanish, French, Italian, Irish, Latin, and Greek. Showing a preference rather ahead of his time, he placed the study of history high on the educational agenda. His special skill, however, was the production of Greek scholars.

As dean of studies, he employed the tool of irony. "The only redeeming trait [of an unsuccessful class]," he once announced, "was that they seemed perfectly ashamed of themselves." With respect to an individual academic failure he remarked: "We admired, though were not altogether pleased with X's coolness while under [oral] examination; during the most interesting part of it, he called his examiner's attention to the meteorological fact that it was snowing."

Father O'Callaghan was

short in stature, with a distinctive hooked nose and small beaming eyes. . . . He was, says a report, "gentle as a lady," and appeared "to be always apologizing for his existence." At times he would actually weep when he felt that his classes were not cooperating with his efforts. He was, however, no weakling. He was a constant participant in the most strenuous sports of the students, and the boys eagerly sought his companionship.

1. The Reverend Robert Plunkett, Georgetown's first president, who served from 1791 to 1793.

2. William Gaston, Georgetown's first student, who served in Congress from 1813 to 1817 and closed a distinguished legal career as a justice on the North Carolina Supreme Court.

3. View of the campus, painted in 1830 by James Alexander Simpson, Georgetown professor of painting and drawing.

4. Old North, built in 1791, Georgetown's second and oldest-surviving building.

5. The President's clock, before which erring students were obliged to stand and study, long stood at the top of the stairs in Old North.

6. An artist's inaccurate conception of a real event—George Washington being received in Old North in 1796. The porch and railing pictured here were a much later addition.

7. A contemporary artist's view of Old South when it was used as quarters by the 69th (Irish) Regiment of the New York State Militia throughout May 1861. President Lincoln came to the campus to review the troops on May 8.

8. Old South, Georgetown's first building, begun in 1788, demolished in 1904.

9. The class of 1858, the earliest class of which a photograph exists.

10. Hoya Saxa! ("What Rocks!") Team! Team! Team

11. A Mathew Brady photograph of Father James Curley, seated in the chair President Lincoln gave the photographer.

12. The Astronomical Observatory, established by Father Curley in 1841.

13. Father Patrick F. Healy, the University's twenty-ninth president, whose development program after the Civil War prepared the way for the modern Georgetown.

14. The Healy Building under night clouds.

15. The Carroll parlor in the Healy Building today. Here are kept the Gilbert Stuart portrait of John Carroll (*frontispiece*), a Van Dyck, and other art and historical treasures.

16. Going to the football
game in the 1890s.

17. The Gibson girl in her
role as Georgetown cheer-
leader.

18. The Hilltop, as photographed by Mathew Brady from the Virginia side of the Potomac.

19. An artist's conception of the Hilltop campus as seen from the Key Bridge in 1889, the Centennial Year.

One of his pupils later pictured him as "a man of medieval rather than of nineteenth-century type." The estimate would be more exact if one were to change "medieval" to "renaissance." The encyclopedic quality of his knowledge recalls the broad yet profound sweep of the typical European mind of that period. He was fascinated by the potentialities of thought, and he relished new intellectual data as a gourmet savors rich food.

Like his colleague, Father Lynch, he devoured English literature, and roundly affirmed that "he would not sit at a desk that had not Shakespeare on it." He was skilled in stimulating his students to original and independent thinking. The boys soon found that they pleased him most when they applied their knowledge to everyday situations and applied it in fresh ways.

In 1868, while crossing the Atlantic, Father O'Callaghan was crushed to death by a table that was thrown against his chest in a storm.

The College was the beneficiary, at this time, of the important services provided by the Jesuit Brothers. These men were, according to the rules of their Order, neither priests nor seminarians, but were engaged in secretarial, general housekeeping, or manual activities in the institution's domestic economy. One historian writes of them: "They performed their various tasks in obscurity and with great competence, and their service was indispensable to Georgetown. They constituted a devoted corps of skilled workers and supervisors, and they can be scarcely praised too highly."

31

The length of service of some of the Brothers at Georgetown is striking. Brother Patrick Sears, dying in 1913 at
the age of ninety-five, was at the College for sixty-two con-
secutive years; Brother James McCloskey for forty-four.
Brother Thomas Dougherty served for thirty-seven years,
Brother Vergil L. Golden for thirty-four.

THE ASTRONOMICAL OBSERVATORY

A highly important event in Georgetown's development occurred in 1841, when plans were laid for the erection of an
astronomical observatory, under the direction of Father James
Curley. With no formal scientific training, Father Curley
seemed to have a sixth sense for the secrets of nature and for
the harmonies of numbers and geometrical forms. There was
something of the joyous play of the child in his mind's sharp
probing of stellar space. He handled mathematical problems
with the dexterity of genius. And, in proof of his virtuosity,
he could turn from investigating the universe and regard
with the eye of a skilled botanist the face of a flower.

He may have been something of a poet. In all his scientific work he gave the impression of touching nature with a
caress. His meticulously detailed notebook records appear to
have been lingered over affectionately, in the mood of a
man tracing the lineaments of a natural world that he
greatly loved.

He had a capacity for unselfish devotion to his pupils,

whose names, long years after they had left the College, he could unfailingly recall.

When Father Curley founded his observatory, there were only two such installations in the United States, those of Williams College and of the Western Reserve College at Hudson, Ohio. Neither the United States Naval Observatory nor the Harvard Observatory was yet in existence. That Georgetown should have had an observatory so early was evidence of Father Curley's remarkable foresight and of his boldness in finance. He sensed that Georgetown had an opportunity to excel in this field of science, and the subsequent history of his observatory has amply justified his instinct. He had the courage to go ahead with his plan in the face of the fact that the College had no money to devote to the project.

The financial lack was met almost providentially. Two of Father Curley's fellow Jesuits were permitted by their superiors to donate to the observatory fund their recently acquired patrimonies, which, being vowed to poverty, they themselves could not accept. About $15,000 was thus assembled, and Father Curley went ahead with the work.

He drew up the plans for the building, supervised the construction, and purchased the astronomical instruments. The three-story brick structure, sixty feet long and thirty feet wide, with a rotating dome, was practically completed by the spring of 1844.

The observatory has been employed primarily for the benefit of the College students, classes in astronomy being regular features of the curriculum. In the present century, post-graduate work has been undertaken and Georgetown astronomers have made distinguished contributions to original research.

In the latter field Father Curley was not idle. He calculated the latitude and longitude of the city of Washington for the first time. Subsequent rechecks of his figures proved them to be almost perfectly correct—a considerable achievement for the mid 1840s, before the advent of more precise scientific aids. Later research accomplishments of the observatory were to bring world renown to this department of Georgetown.

THE ITALIAN ÉMIGRÉS

Toward the close of the 1840s the College was the beneficiary of the anticlerical revolution in Italy. A group of Italian Jesuits, expelled from their native country, sought a new home at Georgetown. Among these learned refugees were several eminent theologians and philosophers and two outstanding men of science. Father Benedict Sestini, astronomer, physicist, and mathematician, was one of the scientists. He had formerly headed the Roman College Astronomical Observatory, and now was to become one of Georgetown's great teachers and scholars. Besides devoting himself to the instruction of the undergraduates, he made an original study of the sun's surface in 1850. The results of this investigation were published by the United States Government, and provided an analysis of sunspots regarded as the most accurate and most comprehensive achieved up to that time. Today Father Sestini is known also for his four textbooks on elementary and advanced mathematics.

Father Angelo Secchi, astronomer and physicist, was at Georgetown only about a year but, during his short stay, was an inspiration to the students. He was later given the directorship of the Vatican Observatory in Rome.

Equally well known, in theological and philosophical circles, were Torquatus Armellini, John Baptist Pianciani, Joseph Ardia, Michael Tomei, Antonio Maraschi, and the Tongiori brothers, Francisco and Salvatore. The addition of such men was a boon to the College.

THE MEDICAL SCHOOL

Georgetown's first professional school was founded in the fall of 1849, the result of internecine strife among local medical men. The Washington Infirmary clinical facilities had been monopolized by a group of District of Columbia physicians and surgeons, and the excluded doctors sought to redress the situation by creating a medical school and infirmary of their own. They requested the president of Georgetown, Father Ryder, to incorporate their school into the College. Father Ryder agreed, and the Georgetown University School of Medicine was born.

The school's first quarters were in a leased building in downtown Washington, on F Street, near Twelfth. Also, a dispensary and six-bed infirmary were erected by the doctors.

The medical school's early history is marked by the coyness of the College directors toward the doctors' financial problems. The Jesuits' attitude on this matter was the standard one adopted by the executive boards of private colleges to which a medical department had been attached.

In brief, the medical teachers paid their own way, with monetary loans (not gifts) from the College whenever the waters became too deep. The president of the College, on the other hand, had a final say in respect to all appointments to the medical faculty and all important policy decisions affecting the school. Technically he even could determine the general nature of the curriculum.

One might ask what the doctors were getting out of all this. In exchange for submission to the College authorities they won the prestige afforded by amalgamation into the corporate structure of a university. Also they could always hope for a loosening of the College directors' purse strings.

FATHER BERNARD MAGUIRE

From August 1852 to October 1858 the College was under the direction of Father Bernard A. Maguire. He was one of the great presidents of Georgetown, although one of the youngest; he began his first term at the age of thirty-four, only a year after his ordination to the priesthood.

Not noted for scholarship, he was magnetic, dominating, and shrewd. He was a strict taskmaster who alternated between sternness and geniality. He could expel six boys in the morning and, that night, sing a song at a student banquet.

While yet a seminarian he had acquired an amazing reputation as an orator, and afterward he won the praise of being "perhaps the most successful missioner on the Continent."

In 1852 he was, wrote James Ryder Randall (a student at the time), "tall, gracefully slender, with black hair aggressively brushed [back] from his ample forehead, and scintillating blue eyes, full of humor and a high state of health. . . . His smile was winning and attractive, but, at times, he could present on his expressive face all of the aspects of a 'son of thunder.' " He was a born actor; he would clasp his hands and dramatically unfold them to punctuate a statement.

Father Maguire directed his school with flair, sound business sense, and a respect for pedagogical values that raised the College in six years to a peak of efficiency never before attained. His gusty, colorful administration, typified perhaps by the smartly stepping College Cadets and the verve of the Philodemic Society, was one of the finest phases of Georgetown's history. He enriched the curriculum, tightened up the examinations, expanded the student organizations, and kept the students at their desks and the faculty on the alert.

THE CIVIL WAR

The Georgetown story during the Civil War years can be told briefly. Like the nation, she survived. Father Maguire put it another way. She was, he said, "nearly ruined." The soldiers of the 69th Regiment, New York National Guard, were billeted for a time in the students' quarters in the early part of the war. President Lincoln reviewed them on the campus on May 8, 1861. They were followed by the 79th Regiment of the same state. After the soldiers came the wounded. The Army Medical Corps took over some of the College facilities in the late summer of 1862.

Students were few during these years, only seventeen on the campus in September 1861 and never more than one hundred. Most of the students and many alumni were fighting the war. One thousand and forty-one Georgetown men —and boys—fought in the tragic conflict, many in blue, more in gray. Georgetown was predominantly a Southern college in those years.

The bloody struggle finally came to an end. The tragedy of Lincoln's death followed, and the Georgetown House Diary recorded the terrible event:

Apr. 14, 1865. In Ford's Theatre . . . the President of the United States was killed by John Wilkes Booth. . . . A crime horrible and never sufficiently to be abominated by all good men.

Georgetown, like the shattered nation, had now to gather herself together and build a future. She did so, again under the leadership of Father Bernard Maguire who, on June 1, 1866, assumed for the second time the presidency of the College. Things at once began to move. Buildings were repaired and enlarged; the campus was newly landscaped and the playing fields expanded; the students—some of them now war veterans—flocked back; and the College resumed its work of imparting education in the liberal arts and sciences. When classes opened in September 1866, there were 180 boarders. By the fall of the following year the number had increased to 250.

Father Maguire noted a change in the character of the student body:

They were more studious, more obedient and they all felt the necessity of hard work. Many of them had spent some years under military discipline and now came to devote themselves to hard work. The [College] Military Companies were again organized and . . . officers took charge of this familiar exercise. We could not depend on the South, now ruined by the reverses of war, and the students were from every section of the country, perfectly united and marching again under the old flag.

It was at this time that Georgetown's official colors were adopted—blue and gray, to signify the union of North and South in one great nation.

39

As always in Jesuit education, much emphasis was placed on the courses in philosophy. A later Georgetown president was to describe the reasons. It is this study, he pointed out, that knits together the various threads of learning and makes of them one consistent and harmonious fabric. The Aristotelian and Thomistic system, he wrote, is a vast, compact, thoroughly reasoned and tested body of philosophic truth, extending over all knowledge. The value of such training for one's whole life and for every profession is incalculable. It induces orderly habits of thought, it maps out and arranges all other knowledge in the mind, and shows the dependence of one field upon another. It gives us our intellectual bearings, affording, in fundamental principles, the points of departure and lines of reference by which all service and all learning is divided and ordered. It develops the power of analysis and supplies the tests by which to judge the results of analysis and induction.

Nor was this all that was happening to the student at Georgetown. "One of the principles underlying all Jesuit education," said Father William Pardow, of the Society of Jesus, some years later, "is that the unit of education is not the college taken as a whole or even the class as a whole, but the individual. . . . St. Ignatius of Loyola in founding his . . . system of education wished . . . the success of his method to be measured by the work done in every single one of those who come under its influence."

FIRST ALUMNI REUNION

On July 2, 1867, the College held the first formal reunion of her alumni. The alumni roster in this year—the golden anniversary of the first graduating class—totaled more than six hundred names, although many of the sons of Georgetown were now deceased. An interesting fact was the large percentage of Protestants among the "old boys." The proportion would be about twenty percent in 1876; and in 1888 the president would declare that one half of the Alumni Association was non-Catholic.

The old graduates revisiting their alma mater in 1867 were requested to bring their photographs for deposit in the College archives. They were treated to much oratory, music, and a gargantuan banquet in the students' refectory. Old Father Curley circulated happily among them, calling them unfailingly by their correct names.

The College commencement of the same year had been attended by President Andrew Johnson and enlivened by music from the 12th United States Infantry Band.

Four months earlier the Medical Department had held its eighteenth commencement, with M.D. degrees awarded to forty-seven men. The total number of medical undergraduates was fifty-eight. This branch of the University was doing a modest though competent work. One of its most important achievements was the large number of doctors it had provided for the nation's armed forces.

A BANNER YEAR

The next-to-the-last year, 1869, of this term of Father Maguire's as Georgetown's head was memorable. During the winter the College Cadets paid a formal visit to President Johnson. Led by the United States 12th Infantry Band (which seemed to be particularly at the service of the College), the boys marched to the White House and were received by the Chief Executive. He favored them with a long address and shook hands with each. The Cadets then repaired to the National Hotel for a multicourse dinner.

The elaborate commencement of that June was an impressive symbol of the school's renewed vigor. President Grant presided and personally distributed diplomas and prizes. Seven Master of Arts degrees were awarded and six B.A.s. "It seemed," a reporter remarked, "as if every State of the Union was represented in the roll of awards [to graduates and to undergraduates for excellence in studies], whilst the gold medal in ethics was awarded to a Mexican."

All the College's resources, oratorical, political, musical, and decorative (the latter supplemented by the attendance of the "female fair"), were enlisted to mark the occasion with splendor. Latin odes and formal addresses—all by the students save one—were directed from the gaily beflagged and beflowered platform to a sturdily receptive audience. In those days a College commencement was not something to be taken lightly. For the ensuing daily and weekly secular press, the Georgetown commencement of 1869 was practically front-page news.

The festivities were marked by a minor diplomatic crisis smoothly surmounted. The son of former President Andrew Johnson was one of the College graduates, and his father was present. Between the latter and President Grant no friendly feelings existed. By a neat directing of the movements of the two, a Jesuit marshal saw to it that they were not forced to meet.

Father Maguire's address on this occasion was interesting for two reasons. First, he was evidently worried by charges against the patriotism of American Catholics. He therefore presented the following meditation on Church-State relations:

Standing here, on the soil that once formed part of the soil of Maryland, *we* do not forget, though others may, that it was the Catholic founder of the colony of Maryland who first on this continent proclaimed the principles of religious liberty, and that the missionaries who accompanied him hither, and gave their countenance and assistance to his work, were *Jesuits*. These principles of religious liberty, of the independence of Church and State (each revolving in its own orbit), we affirm and maintain, and shall ever affirm and maintain.

Both as patriots and as Christians, we should feel it our duty to oppose the establishment on the soil of our common country of a State religion, were it our own or any other. I make these assertions within hearing of the public . . . with the perfect confidence that in what I assert . . . I compromise no member of my order, and no member of the Catholic Church at large.

The second important statement by Father Maguire proclaimed that in the following September Georgetown would open a School of Law.

PATRICK HEALY IN COMMAND

Georgetown as a university may be said to have really begun in the late 1870s. The advance was effected mainly by a man and a building. The man was Patrick Healy, and the building was the structure that bears his name.

Father Healy took hold of Georgetown's affairs in 1868, when he became prefect of studies of the College. His personality is one of the most impressive in the institution's annals.

He was born in Georgia, the son of a Negro bondwoman and a Connecticut sea captain. Mrs. Healy had been a household servant on a plantation with which Captain Healy had business relations. Attracted by the refinement and virtuous character of the young woman, Healy bought her freedom and married her. They settled in Georgia and raised seven sons and three daughters.

Father Healy, nicknamed "The Spaniard" by the students, was tall and handsome, with a trace of the hidalgo in his sweeping gestures and somewhat imperious speech.

He was sociable with people of almost all walks of life. He would strike up a conversation with a stranger in a railway train and, in the process, insert a word of priestly encouragement. Once, when introduced to a young actress who was a Catholic, he gave her a little lecture on her duty to reflect credit on her Church by her personal behavior.

As an educator and university administrator he thought in large, daring, and progressive terms. He set his sights on the highest excellence and was incapable of any conception that was narrow, or any mode of execution that was not thorough. He had a sense of the ever-changing nature of educational problems, and was eager to try new solutions.

If he had a fault, it was perhaps a touch of ruthlessness in directing his co-workers toward the desired ends. A perfectionist himself, he could be caustic in spurring on the less energetic or the mediocre.

STRESS ON SCIENCE

Besides maintaining the academic improvements made by Father Maguire, Father Healy did more. Aware of the great attention accorded to scientific studies in the country generally, he installed at Georgetown science courses which, in extent and intensiveness, went far beyond what was being done in most other American liberal arts colleges.

By 1879 Georgetown was requiring, as a requisite for the A.B. degree, a two-year course in chemistry. Classes in this subject (consisting of sophomores and juniors) met thrice weekly, and each school year comprised about thirty-five working weeks.

This was at least twice as extensive a program as the corresponding course at New York's Columbia College, where students were obliged to attend weekly lectures in a general chemistry course during only one academic year consisting of about five working weeks fewer than that of Georgetown. And the Columbia course in chemistry, according to the president of that college, awarded more time to the subject than did Harvard College (where the subject could, on account of the elective system there in vogue, be completely bypassed); Yale and Williams had chemistry courses equal in length to Columbia's; the average American college, the president of Columbia implied, was giving to chemistry considerably fewer class hours than this.

Georgetown's course in chemistry covered the inorganic and organic fields. Each day's lesson was fully illustrated by the professor with experiments. On the following day, before the new lesson was given, the work of the previous day was rehearsed by the students, minus the experiments. All, however, took turns periodically in performing laboratory work in the presence of the professor. Two examinations, one oral, the other written, were imposed at the expiration of each term of the academic year. No student was promoted to the next scholastic grade unless he had successfully passed these examinations.

A two-semester course of six hours weekly in physics was obligatory for all seniors at Georgetown. (At Harvard, owing to the elective system, a student could graduate if he had had no course in physics.) Moreover, concurrently during the first semester of the senior year, mechanics was studied, with three hours of class weekly; in the second semester of the same year, three classes per week were held in geology and several lectures in astronomy and botany.

For graduation, a written and oral examination in physics, and two similar examinations in mechanics, had to be passed. The oral examinations were individual and private, each student undergoing his ordeal alone with a professor. The written test consisted usually of a single complex topic, assigned on the day of the examination.

The heavy stress placed on the scientific subjects at Georgetown is illustrated by the proportionate time awarded to these final tests. Four of the six major examinations at the senior year's end were in physics or mechanics or other natural sciences. Only two were devoted to philosophy. Graduates were accepted into the junior year of the engineering schools of Cornell, Stevens Institute, and M.I.T.

Supplementing this scientific curriculum was the Toner Circle, a society devoted to field work in geology, botany, and other natural sciences. Founded in 1876, this organization held regular bimonthly meetings for the reading of student scientific papers.

One of these essays, "A Contribution to the Archeology of the District of Columbia," by undergraduate Louis H. Kengla, evoked commendation from the District Anthropological Society.

The Toner Circle was in touch with Thomas Edison, and one day the boys proudly displayed a gift sent to them by the inventor—a dozen Edison electric bulbs and a dozen carbonized fibers for experimental purposes.

Not to be outdone by their more scientific-minded classmates, a student group produced in December 1872 the first number of the *Georgetown College Journal*. Written, edited, and for several years set up in type by the undergraduates, the *Journal* was evidence of their maturity of thought. The quality of Georgetown student writing in this period was never surpassed and not always equaled by twentieth-century articles, stories, and poems in the same *Journal*. It was one more indication of the impetus given Father Healy to the intellectual life of the College.

In his academic reforms, Father Healy was aware that statements of policies and programs were not enough; the essential thing was that they be practiced, and he closely supervised the daily work of the classrooms.

With one assistant, he personally examined in mid-1870 all the classes of the College and some of those of the "preparatory" division. He himself had designated the subjects of all the written themes for the examinations. The minuteness of his observations is seen in this typical summary of the academic performances of Division B of the class of "third humanities":

James Tracey preserved an even and steady pace throughout the entire course and arrived at the goal first. Caldwell Robertson lost and regained his ground by turns and came panting close upon the victor's steps. . . . Frank Repplier started well in the three grammars, stumbled badly in Nepos, but recovering his equilibrium, pushed on with undiminished speed, occupying the fourth position. James McSherry, starting well in his grammars, distanced, by two works, all competitors, fell heavily three times in translation, but, redeeming much by his parsing, occupied the fifth place.

The quality of the work of a college is indicated by the ratio of graduates to matriculants. The graduating class of 1874 had had thirty-seven members in the freshman year; twenty-one survived to receive degrees. The class of '75 was sixteen in number, and had totaled twenty-two sophomores. If we delve more deeply into the history of the graduating classes the statistics are even more striking. The graduates of '75 had lost six-sevenths of the number constituting their class when it was third grammar—roughly equivalent to our present sixth grade of primary school. The graduating class of '76 had lost five-sixths or more of their original number, while the next year's mortality was about seventy-five percent.

AFTER GRADUATION

As to the later results of the College training, to what extent did Georgetown graduates achieve success in their careers? The general estimate made by the *History* appears to be correct: "Of the total number of the alumni, the proportion who were 'making good' in their business or professions, and attaining considerable prominence in restricted localities, surpassed by a comfortable margin what could reasonably have been desired." This rather cautious statement says in effect that the achievements of the typical Georgetown graduate were creditable, but limited in scope; if he did not set the world on fire he made a fair blaze.

A number of Georgetown men became editors, owners, or managers of newspapers or magazines. William S. Walsh was editor of *Lippincott's Magazine* in the late 1880s. John Brisben Walker was the owner of *The Cosmopolitan* in 1891. Robert J. Collier, A.B. '94, became editor and owner of *Collier's Weekly*. Condé Nast, A.B. '94, was for a while the business manager of the same magazine and later founded *Vogue*.

The bench, bar, and politics drew to their services a large proportion of the graduates of the College and the Law School. The Church, business, and medicine, approximately in that order, were the next most frequent preferences of Georgetown graduates.

It was to be hoped, of course, that the Georgetown College alumnus would continue to cherish an affection for the Latin and Greek classics. It is not absolutely certain, however, that rumor was accurate when it represented the oldest living graduate of 1893 as reciting from memory, without a pause, 759 lines of the *Aeneid*.

The quality of a college course may be measured, to an extent, by the number of A.B.s who go on for higher studies. The following is Georgetown's record in this respect during four sample years:

The graduating class of 1890 consisted of eight A.B.s and

four M.A.s; of these, seven are recorded as studying at professional schools other than Georgetown, and one at Georgetown Law.

The graduating class of 1892 consisted of ten A.B.s, eight M.A.s, two Ph.D.s, and one Bachelor of Music; of these, there are records of seven in advanced or professional studies, either at Georgetown or elsewhere.

The graduating class of 1893 consisted of sixteen A.B.s, eight M.A.s, and one Ph.D.; of these, there are records of fifteen in advanced studies, including two at Georgetown Medical School and four at the Georgetown School of Law.

The graduating class of 1894 consisted of fourteen A.B.s; of these, thirteen pursued advanced studies, including one in the Georgetown postgraduate course. (Three later became Jesuit novices.)

The average number of graduates from the College during the period 1885 through 1895 was 15.5.

THE HEALY BUILDING

If Georgetown was to become a university worthy of the name, Father Healy saw, she must have more ample and more modern physical accommodations for her students and for her academic services. Other American colleges were offering to their matriculants comfortable living quarters and up-to-date facilities for study. Georgetown had been suffering some deficiencies in these respects.

Father Healy, with characteristic boldness, determined to erect a structure that would fulfill all these needs. It would be no ordinary building. It would symbolize, by its amplitude and its beauty, the aspirations of Georgetown toward educational achievement on the highest levels.

This is what, within two years, he accomplished. Starting with practically no financial reserve, he borrowed, sold almost half the College's real estate, and economized on ordinary expenses, conjuring up approximately $200,000 for his project. By 1878, although he broke his health in the process, he had raised on the Georgetown campus a structure that to this day is a monument to a great ideal of culture. The Healy Building, as it was named against his wish, gave to Georgetown the physical basis for expansion.

AN IMPORTANT STEP FORWARD

In 1876 the medical faculty was almost completely reorganized and expanded. Some of the older doctors—whose services to Georgetown can never be forgotten—were retired and new physicians and surgeons added to the teaching staff.

Two years later occurred a major revision of the Medical School curriculum. This improvement has been described by a later dean of the school as being "the brightest event in the history of the [Medical] College." The period of study required for a degree was increased from two years to three, with the duration of each individual course increased to seven months instead of the previous five.

This was an innovation that placed Georgetown's Medical School in a select group. By 1880 so great a lengthening of the course had been adopted by only eight of the 128 medical colleges in the United States and Canada. In 1885 only fifty-two of these schools out of a total of 233 were offering courses as long as six months.

The evidence suggests that this department of the University was doing a competent teaching job. The school was not, however, engaging to any important extent in research; few medical colleges at the time were doing so. Richard H. Shryock, in his *American Medical Research: Past and Present,* points out that research in the field was "just getting under way" as late as 1895.

Applying the customary yardstick, a public health official congratulated the school on "the small percentage of . . . graduates to matriculate" and on "the other marks of improvement." The commendation seems to have been well deserved. With an average enrollment of eighty students through the period 1870–1900, the average number of degrees granted each year was twenty-three. The record for some of the years 1877–1883 inclusive is even more interesting:

1877–78	40 students	4 graduates
1878–79	38 "	6 "
1880–81	43 "	5 "
1881–82	30 "	7 "
1882–83	27 "	4 "

GEORGETOWN'S DOCTORS

Of the doctors and physicians on the school's faculty, five deserve special mention. Doctor Joseph Tabor Johnson, professor of obstetrics and diseases of women and children, had studied in Europe under the great Doctor Karl Braun of Vienna and was one of the founders of the American Gynecological Society. He was the author of part of Dennis' *American System of Surgery* and Reed's *Gynecology*.

Doctor Samuel C. Busey, professor of theory and practice of medicine, was a charter member of the American Gynecological Society, the American Pediatric Society, and the Association of American Physicians. In 1890 he was elected president of the last-named body.

Doctor Thomas Antisell taught chemistry and toxicology at the school, and was the author of many learned articles in these fields. During his professorship at Georgetown he acted also as chief chemist for the United States Department of Agriculture.

Doctor Francis A. Ashford was the leader in the movement that founded the District of Columbia General (Garfield) Hospital in 1881. With Doctor Busey, he had established the local Children's Hospital in 1870.

Doctor George Tully Vaughan made fame for himself and the school by his operations on the heart for gunshot injury and for the transplantation of joints. Doctor George M. Kober, a later dean of the school, believed that Vaughan

20. Marshal Foch, commander in chief of the Allied armies in World War I, being formally received on the porch of Old North.

22. The last cracking of the book before class; in the background the John Carroll statue and the Healy Building.
Photo by Peter Carter

21. Perspective from the White-Gravenor terrace.
Photo by Peter Carter

23. Secretary of Commerce Herbert Hoover on the platform, June 1926, after receiving an honorary degree.

24. Governor Alfred E. Smith walking in the academic procession of the 1941 commencement exercises.

25. Mask and Bauble, the College dramatic society, promotes a play.
Georgetown University News Service. Photo by Bob Young, Jr.

26. Bob Hope, featured speaker at a banquet in New South Hall.
Georgetown University News Service. Photo by Bob Young, Jr.

27. Eugenio Cardinal Pacelli received on campus in 1936 upon being awarded a Georgetown degree.
Photo by Harris & Ewing

28. Pope Pius XII welcoming Georgetown delegation in the Vatican.

29. Field Mass at Fort Meade, Maryland, for Georgetown ROTC members on maneuvers.

U. S. Army Photograph

30. Military Prize Competition Day. On the upper right stands the new Science Center.

Photo by Peter Carter

31. Healy's spires reflected in the old Chesapeake and Ohio Canal, of which George Washington was an original promoter and stockholder.

32. Father Edmund A. Walsh, vice-president of Georgetown and regent of the pioneering School of Foreign Service, which he founded.

33. President Dwight D. Eisenhower arriving in October 1958 to speak at the dedication of the Walsh Memorial Building. He is greeted by Father Edward B. Bunn, Georgetown's president, and Patrick A. O'Boyle, Archbishop of Washington.

Georgetown University News Service. Photo by Bob Young, Jr.

34. A view of the stacks in the Riggs Memorial Library, Georgetown's central library.

Georgetown University News Service. Photo by Bob Young, Jr.

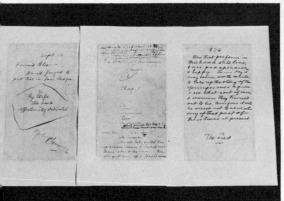

35. Pages from the Library's many treasures — the manuscript of *The Adventures of Tom Sawyer*.

36. Baccalaureate Mass, the formal beginning of the annual commencement exercises.
Georgetown University News Service. Photo by Bob Young, Jr.

37. Under the late afternoon sun of a June day, hundreds of Georgetown students receive their degrees. Father Edward B. Bunn, the University president, is speaking.
Georgetown University News Service. Photo by Bob Young, Jr.

"was the only surgeon in this country who transplanted a knee-joint."

Two other surgeons of more than ordinary ability—Doctors Johnson Eliot and John B. Hamilton—were teaching at Georgetown during this period. The former had in 1870 or 1877 performed an operation for aneurism, a rare achievement at the time.

In 1888 Doctor Hamilton's operation on a man who had been shot in the abdomen was said by Doctor Joseph Tabor Johnson to be one of the most skillful he had seen.

One of the most colorful of the District's medical men was Doctor James Kerr, professor of surgery at Georgetown for several years, beginning in 1892. He had a habit of throwing instruments around in the operating room whenever anything displeased him. The medical historian Doctor Philip Caulfield makes the following defense of his colleague: "It seemed that Doctor Kerr was no different from most surgeons of that era, for all seemed to delight in this pastime. Whether this was due to temperament or to pressure of their work or to the combination of both is unknown. It was probably the latter with a touch of showmanship thrown in."

TEACHERS OF LAW

The Law School, no less than the Medical School, found in Father Healy's leadership a new source of energy in its development. From its original location in a rented room in the Colonization Building in downtown Washington, it had moved in 1872 to larger quarters in a part of the old Washington Catholic Seminary structure a few blocks away. It had only thirty-one students in 1876, and its total income for 1872–1874 was $278.76, but it was growing.

If the Law School was a meager operation financially, there was nothing second-rate about its faculty. Between 1870 and 1874 the students heard regular lectures from Justice of the United States Supreme Court Samuel F. Miller. (Two other Justices were to teach at Georgetown— Stephen J. Field in 1885–1886 and Henry B. Brown from 1891 through 1894.)

Another notable Georgetown law teacher at this time was Charles P. James, an associate judge of the Supreme Court of the District of Columbia and a pioneer in the study of statutes. In 1866 he had served with Caleb Cushing on the commission for the revision and consolidation of the Statutes of the United States. Judge James supervised the 1875 and 1877 editions of the newly arranged Federal Statutes. Another achievement was his scholarly historical essay on Congress' power to punish for contempt.

The onetime Assistant Attorney General of the United States, J. Hubley Ashton, said of James: "It was during and as a result of this work [of codification of the Federal laws] that [he] acquired that power he had of understanding at a glance the true and full legal meaning of a series of statutes of more or less difficult construction, a power which he possessed in a more eminent degree than any lawyer whom I have ever known."

As a result of Father Healy's reshuffling of the Law School faculty, Judge Richard T. Merrick came to Georgetown. He had won national prominence by his pleas before the Hayes-Tilden Electoral Commission. No member of the District of Columbia bar was more influential.

Also lecturing at the school during the 1870s were Halbert E. Paine, author of the standard textbook *Paine on Elections* and, during 1878–1880, United States Commissioner of Patents; and George W. Paschal, a prolific writer on legal subjects and editor of the *Annotated Constitution*.

ALUMNI FORMALLY ORGANIZED

The last step taken by Father Healy in his efforts to make Georgetown a university was his gathering of the alumni in a formal organization. It was hoped that the older sons of Georgetown would indulge themselves not only in nostalgic recollections but also in financial contributions to alma mater. The Society of the Alumni held its first annual meeting in May 1880 and encouraged its sponsor by issuing this statement:

Our Alma Mater, up to this time . . . has received nothing whatever from her students except their tuition fees, with which modest means indeed wonders have been effected. But she imperatively needs something more at this time to carry forward her progress. . . .

Father Healy in 1878 added to the law curriculum a post-graduate course of one year. This was an example of fore-sight, since, according to the historian of American legal education, advanced programs of study were undertaken by few of the nation's law schools until the third decade of the present century.

FUNDAMENTAL GOALS

The College during these years—as throughout her history —was striving to maintain what James Bryant Conant has called "some continuing contact with those fields in which value judgments are of prime importance." The Georgetown Jesuits would agree with Conant's view that "the student . . . in college and in graduate school must be concerned, in part at least, with the words 'right' and 'wrong' in both the ethical and mathematical sense."

More socially oriented, President Truman's Commission on Higher Education for Democracy made substantially the same point. "Today's college graduate," declared the commission in 1947, "may have gained technical or professional training . . . but is only incidentally, if at all, made ready for performing his duties as a man, a parent, and a citizen. Too often . . . he falls short of that human wholeness and civic conscience which the cooperative activities of citizenship require."

These things also were what Georgetown was trying to give to her students, as the *History* points out:

She taught that a man should live according to moral principles based on the Christian religion; and she plainly and forcefully specified what she deemed these principles to be. She taught that a man should not only be free, but also dutiful. Liberty was valuable, but so was a personal sense of responsibility.

Under Father Healy's successor, Father James A. Doonan, the two professional schools were moved to more appropriate quarters. For the Medical School, an entirely new building was constructed and ready for occupancy in 1886. The Law School in 1884 left its original location and leased a remodeled structure at the corner of Sixth and F Streets. Not until 1891 would the school own its physical plant.

The Medical School's dissecting room was situated in downtown Washington. Surrounding this theater of gory activities were business houses, residences, and St. Joseph's Orphanage for boys.

One day in mid-November of 1888 a persistent, powerful, and putrid smell pervaded the neighborhood. The reaction of the neighbors was immediate. They demanded that the District Board of Health remove the source of the nuisance. In addition to the odor, protested the outraged citizenry, there was the succession of shocks sustained by the children of St. Joseph's when, through the orphanage windows, they beheld—as they scarcely could avoid doing—the corpses stretched out on the dissecting-room tables.

The storm of complaints was assuaged neither by a health

officer's remarkable statement that "a dissecting room is as healthy as a parlor," nor by the Georgetown doctors' insistence that they had an efficient device for controlling the smells that were inseparable from medical instruction of this kind. The smell, as the neighbors pointed out, was still there.

It was finally discovered that an employee had neglected to operate the odor-suppressing facility. The Georgetown spokesman added that a special problem had recently arisen in the form of an unusually overripe cadaver. The affair, and the smell, soon blew over.

STUDENT LIFE

Student life at the College during the 1880s showed little change, although there were some signs of a growth in maturity on the part of the boys. The *College Journal* carried a reference to "our dudes," with "their silver-headed canes, sporting hats, and . . . spring overcoats carried gracefully over their arms." And some of the students attended a dancing class in Washington: the grim truth was that not until 1904 did "mixed" dances become a feature of undergraduate social life. (This appears to have been the case with American colleges generally.) A sign of increased independence was the adoption of tobacco chewing by some of the boys.

Intercollegiate athletics were becoming a preoccupation of

the nation's youth, and the Georgetown boys enthusiastically followed the trend.

On May 10, 1870, Georgetown's first intercollegiate baseball contest was played against the team from Columbian College. The latter won by a score of 23 to 17. Seeking revenge the following October 25, the Georgetown boys were again set back, to the tune of 30 to 16. It is clear from these statistics that in this era of the game's development the defense was somewhat inferior to the offense. In fact, this October encounter was an even more impressive example of batting strength than it sounds, since the game was called in the sixth inning on account of darkness. Rallying bravely, the Blue and Gray nine proceeded to whip the Columbian team in two successive meetings. By the late 1880s Georgetown was competing in baseball, with fair success, against the Naval Academy, University of Virginia, Johns Hopkins, and several local amateur clubs.

So successful was the Georgetown baseball team in 1887 that the *College Journal* issued the following warning:

We understand that the next game to be played is with the Agricultural College of Maryland. It is to be hoped that our College friends from Maryland will present a much stronger team than that which the [Georgetown] nine has encountered thus far; for, if victories continue to come so easy, it will only be a short time until the boys will think themselves invincible, and such a state of affairs would be deplorable.

Temptation to pride was forestalled when, shortly afterward, the Olympics, an amateur club of the District, defeated Georgetown in two successive games, 20 to 16 and 8 to 3.

On the other hand, it appeared that at least one Georgetown player was modest to a fault. "Our best pitcher," reported the *Journal* in January 1878, "did not discover, until informed by others, that he was throwing curves."

Georgetown played her first football game against an off-campus rival in 1887. The identity of the opponent is not recorded. The following year the College played against the moderately strong teams of Alexandria High School and Emerson's School.

Intercollegiate competition in track and field sports also was becoming an interest of the College students, although Georgetown's great days in this area would not arrive until the late 1890s.

The College Boat Club had been organized in the late 1870s "on the bold supposition," a historian remarks, "that they might engage in intercollegiate competition in this line." The same historian recounts the vicissitudes of the Boat Club: "After securing, in this order, a constitution, an executive committee, a large and beautiful banner, a boathouse, three boats, and, last of all, a crew, the organization had by 1880 foundered on the rocks of financial stringency."

From this effort derived one of the classic songs of the college:

Give way—give way—no man shall say
We're laggards at the oar;
No dame shall flush, nor maiden blush,

For Georgetown's honest fame.
Hurrah! then, boys, hurrah! hurrah!
The Blue and Gray forever.

Uniting the intellectual with the athletic, funds (though not enough) were raised for the Boat Club by "Literary Readings" presented by the students to the public at fifty cents a head.

PRIORITY FOR SCIENCE

Scientific studies in the College continued throughout the 1880s in a position of priority. Besides the large amount of time allocated to classroom and laboratory work in chemistry, physics, mechanics, astronomy, and other natural sciences, much extracurricular and voluntary work was being done by the students in these fields.

The papers written by members of the Toner Circle proliferated. They discussed such topics as "The American Deer's Horns" and "The Anatomy of the Digestive Apparatus." An essay entitled "The Introduction of the Domesticated Reindeer into Alaska" stressed the beneficial results for the human inhabitants. The Circle membership debated in 1877 the possibility of electricity ever being used as a mechanical power, and decided the question correctly. They even showed foresight in concluding that the balloon would not be the most favorable vehicle for air travel and that machines would supersede skilled labor. While they would sometimes lapse into less relevant speculations, such as this one: "Would the Flooding of the Sahara Desert Bring Economic Benefits?" they confined their investigations mainly to current topics of scientific interest.

Directing the Circle's activities during the late seventies and early eighties was a young Jesuit (not yet a priest), a future president of Georgetown, J. Havens Richards. He was ideally suited for inspiring in boys a love of original thinking in science. Although an amateur, he had already executed physics experiments that were remarkably advanced for the times. When Thomas Edison was trying to find a suitable filament for the incandescent electric light bulb, Richards was working on the same problem and maintaining a correspondence with Edison. The inventor had even sent to the eager seminarian some experimental materials.

What is more surprising, Richards had designed an original device for magnifying the sound in telephone transmitters. In doing so he was anticipating an invention that the Bell Telephone Company did not succeed in producing until 1931.

Another inspiration for scientific researchers was the durable Father Curley, who in 1885 celebrated his eighty-ninth birthday. His curiosity about natural phenomena was as keen as ever. In order to determine how rapidly a fingernail would grow, he left his own uncut for a month and daily measured its length:

After dinner in recreation [he records in his diary] we measured it from the morning of the 9th of Feb. to 1 P.M. today, 29½ days . . . The growth was 0.147 (about 1/7 of an inch) long, making 1½ in. in a year.

He was fond of demonstrating his experiment with acoustic figures:

Sprinkling . . . sand lightly on one of his metallic plates of various shapes, then touching the edge with his violin bow and always causing a different musical note, he made the sand dance into a variety of geometrical figures as perfect as the rule and compass could make. . . . When wonder was expressed, he said he had been practicing [the experiment] for forty years.

When old students revisited the College, Father Curley was usually able to recall not only their own first names but those of their fathers or grandfathers. Only rarely would his memory fail him, as witness this entry in his diary for 1887: "On the 19th Thomas Tasker Gant of St. Louis called here. He and his brother were students here in 1831, 56 years ago. . . . I remembered them but could not recognize him. He is 73 years old."

PHILOSOPHICAL DISPUTATIONS

In the college of the 1880s the philosophical and literary subjects were receiving their share of attention. On a day in 1883 many voices apparently raised in anger could be heard in the auditorium. Fists were banged on desks, feet were stamped, and cheers of a vigorously partisan nature were shouted. This was not the beginning of another of George-town's rather stylized student riots. It was a philosophical disputation.

A student chosen for outstanding scholarship was seated on the platform. His duty was to defend theses of scholastic philosophy against objections offered by the audience. What made his task difficult was the fact that most of the attacks on the Scholastic positions came from members of the Jesuit faculty—and their objections were not mere formalities or straw men, but real and not easily met. The "defending" student was forced to do some highly original and independent thinking if he was not to lose the argument. The procedure was not a poor way of training the young men for the rough give-and-take of discussion of basic issues. More than one graduate testified years later how much this kind of education had influenced his business or professional life.

COLLEGE JOURNAL

That the College students were not being unduly censored when they wrote for their *Journal* is evidenced by some of the articles printed. One article, awarded a prize by the faculty, launched a vigorous attack against the prominence given to the Latin and Greek classics in college education. The Jesuits gave a medal also to the author of a piece hailing the new Catholic University of America (founded in

1889) and strongly implying that it was time the nation had a *real* Catholic institution of higher studies!

While a conservative American public was expressing its shock at Oscar Wilde's recently published *Picture of Dorian Gray*, a *Journal* student reviewer calmly unburdened himself of the following: "Wilde is a man of such an original and audacious turn of mind that the commonplace is scarcely possible to him, and so he has produced a novel entirely out of the ordinary ruts."

It would be inaccurate, however, to say that the *Journal's* literary critics always made sound judgments. One of them lived to blush at his statement that the style of Lincoln's Gettysburg Address was banal, while Everett's speech on the same occasion was a masterpiece.

Such slips are easily forgiven when one reads another item in a later *Journal*—the printing of an address spoken by a Georgetown M.A. graduate. Certainly the young man was far ahead of many of his elders in his perception of social realities:

He [the Christian lawmaker] will listen to the cry of the laborer for short hours and more work. . . . While keeping the State to its proper functions, he can countenance laws that will anticipate [i.e., preclude] strikes . . . and encourage associations to better the condition of the working man. This [Christian] principle will teach the employer not to look on wage earners as mere chattels . . . but in the light of men and Christians. . . . [The employer] will be prompted to listen to fair arbitration, and cheerfully grant to labor the remuneration that decent frugality and reasonable comfort demand.

CENTENNIAL CELEBRATION

On February 20–22, 1889, Georgetown University celebrated the centennial year of her founding. The festivities were climaxed by a solemn academic convocation attended by President Benjamin Harrison, Secretary of State James G. Blaine, Cardinal Gibbons, and other dignitaries. Forty-eight honorary degrees were conferred while a determinedly patient audience looked on.

The three days' proceedings were conducted with "dignity, splendor, and pomp that never became pompous." Overindulgence in nostalgia was avoided by such devices as periodic bursts from strategically-placed government artillery and, particularly, by the orators' stress on Georgetown's future as well as her past.

Father Doonan, in his sermon at the Pontifical Mass, said that while Georgetown was "tenacious of the results and well-tried methods of the past," she had also "high hopes and far-reaching aspirations for the future development and broadening of her sphere of activity." He recalled that John Carroll had laid down the broad lines of Georgetown's educational work "not in narrow-minded adherence to old forms and methods"; and, Father Doonan implied, this would continue to be the University's aim.

This position was echoed by Daniel J. Geary, of the College graduating class, who urged that the best thing to do was to "present the old truths . . . not in the old way, but with . . . freshness, with the vigor of a newborn idea." A symbol of this progressive traditionalism was the bedecking of the Old South Building with Edison's newly invented multicolor electric lamps.

OBSERVATORY UNDER HAGEN

Georgetown began her second century of accomplishment by reinvigorating her Astronomical Department. Soon after assuming the presidency of the University in August 1888, Father J. Havens Richards had secured the transfer to Georgetown of the internationally known astronomer-mathematician Father John Hagen. This scholar had won recognition in scientific circles by his series of articles on variable stars published in the Harvard Observatory Annals. He had also collaborated in investigating the same problem with the director of the Lick Observatory in California.

Father Hagen's presence at Georgetown at once began to be felt. The observatory was renovated, and an important addition made to the equipment—a twelve-inch equatorial telescope of superior quality. "When it is remembered," declared a Detroit newspaper, "that this instrument . . . compares notably with the working glasses of any of the more famous observatories of the country . . . the importance of the contribution to the working forces of American astronomical observatories may be understood."

During Father Hagen's first year at Georgetown the first volume of his monumental *Synopsis der Hoeheren Mathematik* was published. This scholarly work, unique in its field, evoked praise from professional journals throughout the world.

The American mathematician W. B. Smith, after pointing out that a great obstacle to original research in mathematics in the United States had been the practical inaccessibility of mathematical literature, declared, "It is precisely such a view as this, minute yet comprehensive, that Professor Hagen has attempted to present; a more useful labor than this in the present condition of mathematical literature can hardly be imagined." Reviews in German, French, Spanish, and other scientific journals termed the *Synopsis* "original in every respect," "colossal in its content . . . truly new in its form."

A second major work from the new staff of the observatory was Father George A. Fargis' *The Photochronograph and Its Application to Star Transits, Georgetown College Observatory*. This monograph was a report by Father Hagen's young assistant, who had just invented an instrument which provided a solution for a problem that had puzzled astronomers for half a century, namely, how to eliminate that greatest of all errors of observation, the "personal equation." The Georgetown astronomer had invented the first practicable instrument for photographing star transits. The Baker-Nunn camera, in use today for star photography, is a development of Father Fargis' device.

Even while the experiments with the photochronograph

were still in progress, another research project had been initiated at the observatory. Astronomers had for a long time suspected that the position in the earth of its axis of rotation was not constant, as formerly supposed, but that it was subject to very slight variations. These are so small that it requires a most refined observation to discover them.

Previous methods had necessitated a correction (by spirit level) of the observation, to compensate for a change in the instrument's horizontal position. To eliminate the need for this correction, Father Hagen floated the telescope on a basin of mercury, and used the photochronograph to adjust the instrument in the meridian and especially to give the scale for the measurement of the plates.

This instrument was constructed in 1893 and mounted in a small frame building connected with the eastern end of the observatory. A set of latitude determinations was made, and the results published.

In 1894 another instrument was invented by one of the research students at the observatory—Father Joseph Algue, S.J., later to attain world fame by his predictions of typhoons. The device was a telescope based on a new principle of reflection. Father Algue took the instrument with him to Manila when he became the director of the Jesuit Observatory there.

THE DAHLGREN CHAPEL

On May 19, 1892, the cornerstone of the new Chapel of the Sacred Heart was laid, with Cardinal Gibbons officiating. The moderate-sized English Gothic edifice, at the west end of the quadrangle formed by the college buildings, was the gift of alumnus John Dahlgren (son of the famous admiral) and his wife. Its cost was about $40,000. "Hither," said the cardinal, "the students will come to implore the God of light to illumine their intelligences and to inflame their hearts with divine love."

THE MEDICAL SCHOOL

For the session of 1891–1892 the Medical School could boast a registration of more than a hundred students. There was a new department of bacteriology, directed by Dr. J. J. Kinyoun, later of the United States Marine Hospital service. A course in pathology would soon be added to the curriculum.

During the summer of 1893 extensive improvements were made in the school's physical plant. Much more space was secured for laboratories. The faculty, explained Father Richards, had learned that the study of bacteriology, histology, and investigations in analytical and practical chemistry required far greater facilities. These it was the intention of the University, aided financially by the doctors, to provide.

One change, however, the Medical School refused to attempt. No women students were accepted. As in the case of all laws of dubious wisdom, an exception was made. An enterprising young woman named Louise Taylor applied for entrance to the school in the fall of 1898. The medical faculty compromised by allowing her to take a special course in anatomy, and she became Georgetown's first coed.

THE LAW SCHOOL

The Law School, at its 1891 commencement, awarded degrees to 112 graduates, representing thirty-two states and territories. The following September the school moved into its new building. The faculty was praised in a contemporary account:

As to the Law School professors, the picture is not only good but remarkable. In the academic session of 1891-1892, Mr. Justice Henry B. Brown, of the United States Supreme Court, was teaching a course on admiralty law; Professor Joseph Darlington's book, *The Law of Personal Property*, had recently been published, and he was lecturing also [at the school] on contracts and negotiable paper; the Honorable William A. Richardson, Chief Justice of the United States Court of Claims, was teaching statutory law; and the faculty was rounded out by five other jurists of outstanding ability, including Martin Morris, George Hamilton, and R. Ross Perry. Tallmadge A. Lambert, about to become Chief Justice of the District of Columbia Court of Appeals, would be added to the teaching corps in the following year, together with the eminent Judge E. F. Dunne. Father René Holaind was lecturing on natural and canon law.

The teaching methods of the Law School followed the views of Woodrow Wilson with regard to legal education, rather than the practically unadulterated casebook technique that had been adopted by most of the law schools of the period. Today's educators are in almost full agreement with Wilson's directive, and have abandoned, for the most part, the exclusive dependence on the case system.

This was the future President's advice, spoken to the American Bar Association's Section on Legal Education in 1894:

He [the undergraduate] should be very carefully grounded in the principles of general jurisprudence before he undertakes to master any particular system of law. . . . The question whether the law, when taught as a profession, should be taught by the inductive use of cases, or by the deductive use of principles already extracted from the cases and formulated in texts is a vexing one. The teaching of law as a profession should no more be irrational than the teaching of it as part of a liberal education or as a preparation for law studies. The case method, therefore, falls short and is slavish if it stops in each instance with the first case in a series. Where did the courts get their principle from in the first case, if there was, indeed, neither statute nor precedent; and if there was a statute, what guided them to its interior meaning? Such are the questions which reveal to the student . . . the real genesis and significance of law. In like manner, the text-book

74

method is neither philosophical nor really instructive unless the principles made use of are challenged, cross-questioned, and made to give a rational account of themselves.

Such a combination method the Georgetown Law School has always maintained.

MORE ADVANCES

From 1894 through 1898 the University had another period of solid achievement. The Medical School inaugurated day classes in 1895; the University Hospital was established in 1898; the Law School added an obligatory third year to its course; the publications of Father Hagen were bringing new prestige to the observatory; the Law School students were highly successful in the new diversion of intercollegiate debating; and—an accomplishment not to be ignored—Georgetown's athletes were winning national (and, in one instance, international) fame.

The reason for the addition of day sessions to the medical course was explained by Father Richards. For some time past, he said, the faculty had been aware that adequate instruction could not be given in the evening alone, especially in view of the wonderful development of medical science of late years.

THE HOSPITAL OPENS

The Georgetown University Hospital received its first patients in August 1898. It was not a large building—sixty by fifty feet and four stories high, with a capacity of thirty-three beds. But it was a sound beginning. It provided more efficient and more convenient clinical and operative facilities for the medical doctors and students, and it satisfied a long-felt need on the part of the district's health services. It was made possible by donations from the public of slightly more than $20,000. The Sisters of Saint Francis, from Philadelphia, were placed in charge.

The hospital was greatly needed, for the Georgetown section seemed to be the scene of more than the average number of accidents. The presence of the terminus of three railway lines within the area, and the dangerous operation of several stone quarries just across the Potomac, probably were responsible. Besides, the hospital was soon called on to care for some casualties of the Spanish-American War.

LAW SCHOOL ADDS THIRD YEAR

The Law School in 1898 made a third year of study mandatory for the degree. In doing so, the school was ahead of the times. Two years after this move by Georgetown, the Association of American Law Schools requested that all its member institutions adopt the same policy before 1905. The proposal evoked bitter debate, many schools protesting that the regulation would mean serious loss. At this time, 1900, only about half of the law schools of the nation had installed the three-year rule.

Although Georgetown's law classes were still held only at night and her entrance requirements were—as in the case of most of her contemporaries—still undeveloped, she had shown, in this lengthening of the course, a notable progressiveness.

INTERCOLLEGIATE DEBATING

The Law School students were winning laurels repeatedly in intercollegiate debates. This form of competition was a product of the nineties and, curiously, an outgrowth of the interest in intercollegiate athletics sweeping the country. At the beginning of the decade, the students of Harvard and Yale had decided that if they enjoyed themselves knocking each other around on the football field, they might derive equal pleasure from intellectual jousts. Teams representing these two schools had staged what appears to have been the first formal intercollegiate debate in 1891. Other colleges soon followed.

The Georgetown law students took eagerly to the new pastime. They started off by defeating teams from Columbian University three times in a row, and during the next six years lost only one contest. Among their victims were the debaters from the University of Wisconsin and New York University.

HAGEN'S ATLAS

Some of the most important original work of Father John Hagen was done during the late 1890s. By the end of the decade he had published his monumental *Atlas of Variable Stars*. The acclaim won by this four-volume production exceeded even the world-wide praise Father Hagen had received for his great book on mathematics.

The publishing history of the *Atlas* included a heartwarming example of cooperation between sister research institutions. When, because of shortage of funds at Georgetown, it seemed that Father Hagen's volumes could not be printed, the obstacle was overcome by a gift of $1750, solicited from a benefactress by the Jesuit's good friend Professor Edward C. Pickering, director of the Harvard University Observatory.

THE NEW CENTURY

Characteristic of the years from 1900 to 1919 was a widespread loosening of the old traditions, moral and religious, on which our civilization has been based. This may have

38.   Aerial view of the hundred-acre campus.
Georgetown University News Service

39.   The Georgetown Yard, heart of the College, whose senior
class president bears the title President of the Yard.
Holmes I. Mettee Studio

40. Celebration of the Liturgy, Byzantine rite, in Gaston Hall.
Photo by Peter Carter

41. Baptist missionaries studying Arabic at the Institute of Languages and Linguistics in preparation for foreign-mission posts.
Georgetown University News Service. Photo by Bob Young, Jr.

42. Language in action—class in the multilingual room.
Georgetown University News Service. Photo by Bob Young, Jr.

43. Astronaut John Glenn speaking to students.
Georgetown University News Service. Photo by Bob Young, Jr.

44. Father Francis J. Heyden at the telescope in the Astronomical Laboratory.

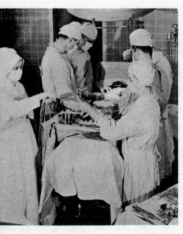

45. Scene in the Georgetown University 400-bed hospital.

46. Summer School registration.
Georgetown University News Service. Photo by Bob Young, Jr.

47. Annual Writers Conference, where editors and free-lance writers meet.
Georgetown University News Service. Photo by Bob Young, Jr.

48. Peace Corps volunteers—cycling is fun on campus and the chief means of transportation in Afghanistan, their destination.
Georgetown University News Service. Photo by Bob Young, Jr.

49. Peace Corps volunteers on lower campus toughening up for overseas assignments to Afghanistan and Iran.
Georgetown University News Service. Photo by Bob Young, Jr.

50. Peace Corps director Sargent Shriver speaking in the Hall of Nations to volunteers training for assignment to Turkey.
Georgetown University News Service. Photo by Bob Young, Jr.

51. Georgetown students (striped uniforms) play American University at soccer.

52. Spirited action on the polo field.
Photo by Peter Carter

53. The crew practicing on the Potomac.
Photo by Peter Carter

54. Training on the board track for intercollegiate meets.
Georgetown University News Service. Photo by Bob Young, Jr.

55. Mrs. Jacqueline Kennedy leaving for her class in American history at Georgetown University as her husband, Senator John F. Kennedy, sees her off. Picture taken March 11, 1954.
United Press Photo

been the price that had to be paid for the freeing of the American mind for more vigorous investigation and experiment. Whatever their faults, the new philosophies of John Dewey and the Behaviorists and the daring image of man presented by the New Literature sent a stimulating current of fresh air through an intellectual America that had in many respects become stagnant. Men were now making mistakes in their thinking, but they were using their minds creatively, and with zest. The viruses of routine, complacency, and fear of change were under attack.

Some men realized that innovation, to be enduring, must be based on the wisdom of those who, throughout the ages, have thought soundly and deeply about matters important to man: Plato, Aristotle, Augustine, Aquinas, Locke. They knew that the fruits of this superior kind of intelligence have been incorporated in the cultural tradition of the West. The Western tradition is a body of thought about man, the universe, and moral values. It sprang from the Greeks, was developed further by Christianity, and has made us what we are today as civilized men. It is, however, a body of ideas and principles that are in no sense inconsistent with reasonable change. It is definite, positive, flatly declarative; yet it can evolve rationally without losing its basic character. It was, in the first decades of the twentieth century, the necessary stabilizer of all attempts to think in fresh and venturesome ways.

The instruction at Georgetown College was providing this steadying influence. In an era of often unwise change she refused to move from the foundations that had formed Western civilization. As her later official spokesmen have expressed it, the College maintained her stand of "the demonstrated philosophical truths about the nature of man, the universe and God; the truths of Christian Revelation and their crystallization through the centuries, including such truths as are expressed in the opening paragraphs of the American Declaration of Independence and are the foundation and principles of the American Constitution and its Bill of Rights."

The College and the University believed in "the Christian culture and conduct having their sources in the teaching and example of Jesus Christ" and in "the opportunity open to all individuals in America for personal initiative, political and religious liberty, and the democratic process of organization." They believed in "the creative development of all human talents through the proper use of liberty, in virtue of the transcendent dignity of the individual moral person and his unique position in the universe." They believed in "the perfectibility of society through the acquisition and practice by its members of the theological, intellectual, moral virtues and their derivatives, such as patriotism, loyalty, and social consciousness; the value of service to the community as an expression of Christian democratic ideals."

HUMANISTIC TRAINING

Moreover, as a part of this education, the students at the College were being trained in humane scholarship. They were being shown the dignity of the word and the harmony of the phrase. The perorations of Cicero rolled sonorously through the classrooms. The nervous, imaged lines of Homer and the massive symbolism of Vergil defined poetic expression. The long clean sweep of Newman's paragraphs were a lesson in prose.

The students were brought in contact with some of the greatest thoughts and feelings that man had ever expressed. Vergil sang of the tears of human things and spoke with serenity of the past. Homer, with reverence and pity, presented man. Horace revealed how tolerance, a sense of irony, and good humor were parts of a civilized attitude.

The students watched with Socrates on the morning of his execution. "There is great reason to hope," he had remarked, "that, going whither I go, when I have come to the end of my journey, I shall attain that which has been the pursuit of my life." They heard Antigone's statement that she feared only one thing—not to die beautifully; and they pondered her paean to the higher laws: ". . . the unwritten and unfailing statutes of heaven; for their life is not of today or yesterday, but from all time, and no man knows when they were first put forth."

They heard the tribute of Pericles to the men who died for their country in battle: "Counting the quest to avenge the City's honor as the most glorious of all ventures, and leaving Hope, the uncertain goddess, to send them what she would, they faced the foe as they drew near him in the strength of their own manhood; and when the shock of battle came, they chose rather to suffer the uttermost than to win life by weakness. . . . They bore on their bodies the marks of men's hands, and in a moment of time, at the climax of their lives, were rapt away from a world filled, for their dying eyes, not with terror but with glory."

They studied the profound and eloquent statements of the Christian view of life: God described by Dante as "the Love that moves the sun and all the stars"; the formula for serenity expressed by the suffering souls in Purgatory, "in His will is our peace"; the Incarnation of God as described by an anonymous fifteenth-century author—"He came al so stille/There His moder was/As dew in Aprille/That falleth on the grass."

BUILDING CONTINUES

In 1903 the Nurses' School was established. A year later the new Kober Operating Amphitheatre provided modern facilities for the surgical department and emphasized steady development by the hospital. The number of beds had increased from 29 in 1900 to 100 in 1903; in 1908 the number of beds was 155; and in 1913 266. In 1908 the Lisner Memorial Building was added to the hospital.

Two new structures arose on the upper campus between 1905 and 1906—the Ryan Dormitory Building and the Ryan Gymnasium—and $10,000 in construction enlarged the Riggs Library in 1907. The Law School had a new building in 1911.

Emphasizing the fact that Georgetown was not based on bricks alone, the College debaters, on April 22, 1904, defeated a team from Boston University amid much ceremonial in Gaston Hall. The first recorded formal dance under the aegis of Georgetown University, the Easter Prom, was held on April 4, 1904. The glittering setting was Rauscher's Auditorium and Hall in downtown Washington. In the same spring the Georgetown Prom was held at the new Willard Hotel.

These affairs were a sign of increasing sophistication in the social mores of the students. Athletic victories in the 1880s and early 1890s had been celebrated in the College yard; the football heroes of 1900 were fêted in the National Theatre. The traditional sedate halftones of the *College Journal* were superseded by student John E. Sheridan's line drawings of the Gibson Girl, the reigning type of feminine beauty.

LORD BRYCE

A graceful compliment was paid to Georgetown at the beginning of 1911 by a famous Englishman. Attending an alumni dinner at the Hilltop in honor of Chief Justice White, Lord James Bryce lauded the College's academic orientation. What the age needed, he declared, was a stress on what he termed the "humanistic" studies, and this, he was happy to see, was Georgetown's emphasis. He liked Georgetown also because it had remained a small college; the all-important liberal arts could be taught best in institutions of smaller size, he believed.

Bryce also spoke feelingly about the Healy tower: "I think the graceful spire that adorns the Healy Building is one of the most beautiful sights in Washington. As I walk out of an afternoon, I frequently pause and admire it, silhouetted against the tender saffron of the sunset sky."

On the same occasion a kind word was spoken for Georgetown by John W. Yerkes, the former United States Commissioner of Internal Revenue. Extolling culture as the motive of education provided in the smaller colleges of the nation, he singled out Georgetown as an example of this orientation. Georgetown, said Mr. Yerkes, was a college where the dollar mark was not imprinted upon its doors—which was true, of course, in a sense not comprehended by the speaker.

THE CHIEF JUSTICE

Chief Justice White eulogized his alma mater in 1912. The occasion was the unveiling of the bronze statue of John Carroll on the front campus. To an audience including Cardinal Gibbons, the Attorney General of the United States, and a galaxy of foreign diplomats, Justice White said:

I never touch anywhere any of the work of the founders of this government that I do not wonder at the marvelous mental proportion which their work displays. When I go to the White House, which lies not far from us, and look at the simplicity and beauty of the proportions of the building I think there could be no greater monument to the wise conceptions of the fathers and their far advancement ahead of their times than is demonstrated by that building which stood for all these years, and today is as fit a habitation for the President of the United States as could be erected if done at this particular moment. So also when I look at this statue and my eye falls upon this building the same thought comes to me. For the rudimentary conception lying at the foundation of the institutions that our fathers founded was the individual—the individual's morality, the individual's judgment, the individual's self-restraint, the individual's devotion to duty, and the individual's love of country. So Carroll, the bishop, in founding Georgetown University, was doing work which joined and bound him up with Carroll, the signer of the Declaration of Independence. In order that the work of the latter might endure it had to be fortified by the work done here; for without the moral principle of the individual, his power to re-strain himself and his willingness to submit himself to the will of the majority, all the principles of the freedom guaranteed by our constitution would pass out of existence. The great conception which evidently lay in the heart and intellect of the bishop when he builded this institution here, was that he was going to organize a great army of morality, which would spread from one end of our country to the other, and at all times and on all occasions be the mainstay and the prop of the institutions which the fathers founded. So as I turn my eye from this statue and this building I see with my mental vision the building upon the Hill. They seem to me one the complement of the other; to me they seem to be one, the necessary resultant of the other; and when the work done here has failed and ceases to produce its effect, the work done there will pass away and our institutions will perish.

DRAMATICS REVIVED

In 1911, under the direction of Mr. Ed Walsh, the College revived an activity that had never been greatly developed there, the theater. The Dramatic Society took on new life. In 1913 Georgetown's first musical comedy was produced for the public—two performances at Washington's National Theatre and another in the Plaza Hotel, New York. Book and lyrics were written by student Edward McTammany Donnelly, College '14, with an all-male cast acting, singing, and dancing out the sentimental joys and woes of Arlette, the Maid of Marchfeld.

A gilt-edge list of patronesses studded the program, including the wives of the English and French ambassadors. Also present at the premiere was George M. Cohan, on his farewell tour in "Broadway Jones."

The operetta was an above-average amateur production and even won a tolerant notice from the New York *Herald*: "College Boys as Chorus Girls Fool Parents: Own Mothers Could Not Penetrate Disguise of Georgetown University Students in Clever Operetta."

STUDENT LITERARY OPINION

The student articles in the *College Journal* in these years testified to the efficacy of Georgetown in forming writers.

Either as an antidote to popular romance or as an example of the broad taste of Georgetown students, an essay in the magazine for December 1913 defends what the author terms "red-blooded" fiction:

"Ever since . . . the cave-man first smote his spouse with the thigh-bone of a mastodon . . . the tale of primitive passion and elemental emotions has never wanted an audience." But, the writer points out, most nineteenth-century American fiction had become "puritanic . . . anaemic, and colorless" and the recent "hard-boiled" school was a needed reaction. "One would not care to trade the memory of Frank Norris' *McTeague* for many memories of daintier and more refined characters. . . . And as for Walt Whitman, who would give us his magnificent camaraderie and his superb singing of the physical man . . . ?" One may note without further comment this less acute judgment of the same author: "There are not many novels of Henry James that could recompense us for the loss of Jack London's *Call of the Wild.*"

The *College Journal* was not the only outlet for the students' independent ideas. The years from 1908 through 1916 were active ones for the debating societies; and the public exhibitions in philosophy kept alive the tradition of vigorous dialectic.

BOARD OF REGENTS

In 1914 an important innovation took place in the University's administrative structure. For many years, American institutions of higher learning had included on their boards of directors eminent—and wealthy—men not directly connected with the field of education, men like Rockefeller, Carnegie, and Huntington.

Georgetown now decided to do the same, and on February 28 she created a Board of Regents. The purpose of the new body was

To bring the Alumni in closer touch with the University, its aims, its needs, and ambitions, to obtain the benefits of their counsel in matters of business direction, and to encourage co-operation in the upbuilding of the University in all its departments. It has been . . . determined . . . to create a permanent committee of laymen to advise with the Faculty and to be known as the Alumni Advisory Committee of Georgetown University.

The earliest extant list of the names of the Regents is that of 1916: John G. Agar, Charles A. De Courcey, George E. Hamilton, Anthony A. Hirst, J. Tabor Johnson, M.D., Ernest Laplace, M.D., John D. McLaughlin, J. Nota McGill, Charles L. Palms, J. Lynch Pendergast, J. Neal Power, James F. Tracey, and Francis X. Anglim, secretary.

This soliciting of the closer collaboration of laymen in University affairs was a forward step which at once began to bring beneficial results.

SPORTS TRIUMPHS

In the years from 1899 through 1916 Georgetown triumphed repeatedly in intercollegiate athletics. Three members of the 1900 football team were named on Walter Camp's mythical "All-Southern" eleven. "Attesting to the fact," writes the *History,* "that a classical education was no deterrent to a sound body, the Blue and Gray footballers of this year played, at one stretch, five games in fifteen days, winning three, tying one, and losing one." At the end of the season they claimed the "championship of the South."

In baseball and track Georgetown achieved a record that brought her into national and international prominence.

The Blue and Gray nine played, during the period 1891–

1900, the leading college and university teams of the East and Upper South. Almost all the great names were on the schedules—Harvard, Yale, Princeton, Dartmouth, Cornell, the University of Pennsylvania, Navy. Of her games against these opponents, Georgetown won, throughout the decade, about seventy-five percent.

In 1899 Georgetown won eighteen out of twenty college games played, defeating within eight days on a whirlwind northern trip the teams of Yale, Harvard, Princeton, Brown, and Wesleyan. The records of the 1900 and 1901 teams against the same kind of high-grade competition were, respectively, twenty-one won, four lost, one tied; and sixteen won, four lost, and one tied.

The 1902 team may have been even better. They beat the professional Washington Senators in two games out of three, and, in the process, Georgetown catcher Lew Drill displayed remarkable versatility. The Senators' management was so impressed that they offered him a contract at once. In the second Georgetown-Washington contest, Drill caught for the Senators.

Perhaps the climax of Georgetown's successes in track came in the summer of 1900. One of her star sprinters, taking up where Berney Wefers, another great Georgetown runner, had left off, went with a select group of American athletes to Europe and won victories at meets in London, Paris, and other cities. This was the famous Arthur Duffy, co-holder with Wefers of the world's record for the 100-yard dash.

The old College Boat Club was reactivated in the spring of 1900. With the financial aid of alumni and friends, an up-to-date eight-oared shell was purchased, a coach hired, and practice begun on the Potomac for an intercollegiate regatta at Poughkeepsie. In June the crew entrained for the meeting on the Hudson, with prudent warnings from the *College Journal* that ". . . much is expected of them at Poughkeepsie, but, of course, as it is our first attempt . . ." They finished the race in last place, but gave, according to observer Walter Camp, "a very creditable initial performance, crossing without collapse."

In the following year the Blue and Gray oarsmen were in the Poughkeepsie race again, and this time gained greener laurels. Although they finished fourth in a field of six, they broke the course record with a time of 19 minutes, 21 seconds. It was the fastest regatta ever rowed in America up to that time, Cornell winning in 18 minutes, 53⅕ seconds. Against competition more suited to their capacities, the Georgetown eight during these years and later won some full-fledged victories. In the spring of 1902 they defeated Annapolis on the Severn; later in the same year, in an invitational regatta held under Georgetown's auspices, the Junior crew finished second in an eight-oared race for Juniors, although the Blue and Gray four-oared shell came in last in the varsity race.

At the Poughkeepsie race of 1903 Georgetown attained her finest hour in major crew competition by coming in second in the eight-oared four-mile race. The *College Journal* was scarcely exaggerating when it termed the Georgetown eight "the tallest, the youngest, the lightest, the greenest crew at Poughkeepsie—the second-best crew in the country."

MASTER SEISMOLOGIST

The work of Father Francis A. Tondorf in seismology won international fame. From 1911 through the 1920s Georgetown set a strong pace in the recording of earthquakes. Amazingly little attention had been given by scientists to the study. "No more than six or seven," Father Tondorf could say in 1916, "of a chain of well-nigh thirty observatories are active in despatching reports . . . of earthquakes recorded."

Later the secretary of the Eastern Branch of the American Seismological Society praised "the work of Georgetown University and of Father Tondorf which did a very important part in keeping alive interest in seismology during a period when there was little encouragement in the form of cooperation and interest on the part of others."

In January 1911, Father Tondorf set up in the basement of the South Tower of the Healy Building a Weishart horizontal and vertical seismograph. The earthquake observatory was made possible by a gift from alumnus Patrick H. O'Donnell, A.B. '92, A.M. '93, LL.B. '94.

Because the Healy tower swayed under heavy winds, the equipment, further modernized, was soon removed to a large cave (12'4" wide, 30'10" long, and 11' high) excavated for the purpose beneath the college quadrangle. A concrete building next to the Astronomical Observatory held a Bosch-Omuri photographic instrument with pendulums of 200 grams each. The time of the occurrence of quakes was automatically registered on these instruments by four contact clocks, corrected by radio signals received from the United States Radiographic Station at Arlington, Virginia.

The function of the observatory was to keep the world informed of the surprisingly frequent upheavals of the earth's crust, and in November 1925 the *Scientific American* wrote, "Our readers will probably realize that most of the items which they see in the daily press with reference to observations of earthquakes . . . will have been made by the Georgetown apparatus."

"'What does Father Tondorf say about it?' That, in substance," wrote H. O. Bishop, Washington *Star* reporter, "is the question flashed by land telegraph, ocean cable, long-distance telephone and wireless from all sections of the world whenever an earthquake tremor is felt. The Associated Press and all the other great news agencies of the world know that they can always depend upon the world-famed Father Tondorf."

One of the Georgetown station's most valuable services was the monthly digest of all press reports of earthquakes and volcanic disturbances. This publication was entitled *Seismological Despatches*, the material being supplied by the Associated Press in return for Father Tondorf's promise to notify that news agency whenever an earthquake was recorded.

On at least one notable occasion Father Tondorf was several hours ahead of the wire services. Early one morning in 1923 he announced to a Washington newspaper that a severe quake had occurred in Japan at about nine on the preceding night. It was then 9 A.M. of the following day and none of the news agencies had received any such information. "You'll hear about it soon," said Father Tondorf blandly; "this one was a whopper." Three hours later, the cables began to quiver with the story of the great Japanese earthquake of September 1, 1923.

Father Tondorf was able to announce in early 1929 the acquisition of a new Galitzin horizontal seismograph, the only earthquake detector of its kind in America. It was said to be the most sensitive instrument in seismic research. Unlike other instruments then in use, the Galitzin type photographed the earth tremors as they were being recorded. With the installation of the new device the Georgetown observatory equipment became one of the most complete in the world.

"The work of your institution's seismic observatory," wrote an official of the Eastern Division of the American Seismological Society to the president of Georgetown on March 3, 1930, ". . . is organized in such a manner and under immediate direction of a sort which is a gratification to all those interested in the progress of seismology."

A special honor came to the Georgetown seismological

department in January 1929. For the first time in history an earthquake recording was sent to Europe by radio, with the cooperation of the United States Coast and Geodetic Survey. Two stations only were included in the message—Honolulu and Georgetown.

WORLD WAR I

War came to the United States in April 1917. The response of Georgetown University was immediate. Before the conflict ended, more than two thousand of the Blue and Gray —students and alumni—were in the nation's armed services. Fifty-four gave their lives for their country.

A unit of the Reserve Officers Training Corps was quickly formed which prepared officers even before the complete mobilization of American colleges under the Students' Army Training Corps in the summer of 1918.

The procedure and curriculum of the SATC were similar to the final plan adopted for the Army Specialized Training Program of 1943—with one notable exception. The student body already on the campus was shifted in its entirety to military status as privates in the Army and assigned to follow a combined military and academic program specified by the War and Navy Departments. Students under eighteen were instructed separately as a civilian unit. The Army and Navy personnel, officers and candidates, at Georgetown amounted to approximately eight hundred. On completion of each three months' period, successful candidates were transferred to regular Army camps for final training as commissioned officers.

Father Edmund A. Walsh, at that time dean of the College, was called to military service by the War Department. He was named Assistant Educational Director of SATC units and assigned to Corps Area #1, comprising some thirty-two colleges in the New England States.

DENNIS P. DOWD

One of Georgetown's proudest stories in connection with her sons' performances in World War I concerns Lieutenant Dennis P. Dowd, College '08. He was the first American to arrive in France from the United States to enlist in the French Foreign Legion. This he did on August 26, 1914.

Later transferring to the 170th Infantry Regiment of the French Army, he was wounded in the Champagne offensive of September–October 1915. When again ready for service he volunteered for the French Air Corps, where he made a brilliant record in training. He was accidentally killed on August 11, 1916, while making his altitude flight.

Nordhoff, Hall, and Hamilton, in their book *The Lafayette Flying Corps,* make this comment: "His loss was an irreparable one to the Franco-American Corps, as it was then called; but coming as it did, when the American attitude toward the Allied cause was still undefined, the news went abroad and did much to enlist American sympathy on the side of liberty-loving nations.

THE SCHOOL OF FOREIGN SERVICE

The war and its aftermath had revealed a glaring defect in the nation's position as a great power—a shortage of expert personnel for diplomacy and international trade careers. The United States, engaging in politics on a world scale and competing in an economic theater of global dimensions, had no training school for the men who would forward her interests in these areas.

Georgetown perceived the challenge, and in February 1919 the first session of the Georgetown School of Foreign Service began. The aim of the courses was to provide the basic knowledge necessary for young men who were to enter the diplomatic service or become employees of private corporations engaged in world trade or international transportation. This aim was stated by its director, Father Edmund A. Walsh, at a convocation of the faculty and students of the school a few months after its founding:

The occasion . . . commemorates the recognition of new problems and the assumption of new obligations by an educational institution whose genius has ever been to conserve the true idea of a university by broadening its scope in response to the growing demands made on human knowledge by the ever-multiplying specialization of man's activity.

A few years later Father Walsh stressed a purpose that was but an extension of an ideal held up by the University as a whole:

. . . Every man who registers in this school [of Foreign Service] must expect to study seriously and constantly the genius of free institutions in order to know the secret of their permanence, resting as they do on the firm basis of the common will freely expressed. . . . You have only learned the real purposes of this school if you . . . present yourselves . . . as living . . . exemplifications of American ideals in government, in business ethics, and rational democracy.

The success of the school was immediate, what with the moral support of the government, the financial aid of private industry, and instruction by a galaxy of expert teachers. The prediction made by a Washington newspaper on the eve of the school's inauguration was soon confirmed:

The classes in foreign trade and government service which open at Georgetown University tomorrow are believed by the government officials to be the most important expression to date of the determination of educational forces of the United States to not only meet the immediate demand, but to intelligently and efficiently train the youth of today to meet the responsibility of tomorrow and so equip this nation to achieve its destiny in the new American era which will be predominated by export business.

Assistant Secretary of State William Phillips offered encouragement: "I want to impress upon you, with all earnestness, that the Department of State is vitally interested in the success of your undertaking. The department wants to co-operate with you, to help you, and to prove to you that it needs in the diplomatic and consular service men who are qualified and trained, as graduates of this school ought to be, for work abroad."

FACULTY

Among the first faculty of the School of Foreign Service were Professor John H. Latané, dean and professor of history at Johns Hopkins University; Dana S. Munro, State Department economist; William F. Notz, chief of the Export Trade Division of the Federal Trade Commission; and the famous expert in constitutional law Westel F. Willoughby.

In 1921 the classes studying international finance and credit were lectured to by Ernest L. Bogart, professor of economics at the University of Illinois, Julius Klein, director of the United States Bureau of Foreign and Domestic Commerce, Stanley K. Hornbeck, United States Far Eastern Advisor at the Paris Conference, Emory R. Johnson, dean of the Wharton School, University of Pennsylvania, and the expert on international law James Brown Scott. Doctor L. S. Rowe, director-general of the Pan-American Union, gave a postgraduate course at the school.

CURRICULUM

The curriculum of the School of Foreign Service has been, from the first, a combination of professional and cultural courses. Established early was an economic and commercial group of lectures including economic resources, commercial development, transportation methods and requirements, public finance, foreign exchange, tariffs, and treaties. The law and political science division presented courses in international and commercial law, the history and principles of American diplomacy, and the history of Europe, Latin America, and the Far East.

Shipping courses, including ocean transportation, ports and terminal facilities, marine geography, steamship accounting, admiralty law, and marine insurance, were also established. There was, finally, a language group comprising studies in foreign tongues, including Japanese, and selected cultural courses.

Today this curriculum has been greatly extended. A marked feature of the school's method is a continual revision of its educational offerings, in accord with ever-changing needs. In 1937, when the Nazis were emphasizing geopolitics, Father Walsh wrote a textbook on that science and introduced it in the school. The study of air transportation, not contemplated by the founder, is now an important part of the curriculum.

Speaking at Georgetown on February 18, 1929, Secretary of State Frank Kellogg paid tribute to the work of the school in preparing young men for diplomatic careers:

The State Department and our country owe a debt of gratitude to this school at Georgetown for blazing the way to a comprehensive [foreign] service training. It is a school now well-known all over the world and it has students from nearly every country.

At about the same time the authoritative journal of international trade, *Export Trade and Finance,* was praising the school's teaching of foreign trade:

There is commendable completeness from the point of view of foreign trade needs in the topics taught, and the teaching personnel seems to be not only unusually competent, but in addition very comprehensive in scope and experience.

One aspect of the school's curriculum noted by the journal had already been attended to by Father Walsh. "The broad and liberal background which assures an intelligent . . . application of technical knowledge to human relations," he declared, "[has been] to a large extent neglected [by American educators]." Hence, the catalogue would soon require "two years of preliminary studies . . . devoted mainly to such cultural subjects as will properly prepare for the more specialized and technical branches of foreign service training."

This, Father Walsh believed, would provide "more leisure for the formation of that liberalized state of mind which should prove the best guarantee for a wise, efficient, and moral administration of the tremendous political and economic power devolving upon the coming generation in America."

INTERNATIONAL CONTACTS

In accord with its slogan, "International Peace Through International Understanding," the school encouraged personal contacts between its students and the Latin American peoples. Summer trips to South and Central American countries were regular features of the students' training.

In the summer of 1920 a Georgetown student group journeyed to Venezuela. That the trip was no mere junket appears from the topics to be investigated by the young men: economic resources, port facilities, transportation, and currency. The results of the students' research were collected in a brochure entitled *Venezuela: An Economic Report Presented by Students of the School of Foreign Service as an Aid to the Foreign Trade of the United States.*

Similar trips were made to Guatemala, Mexico, and other countries to the south, and in 1923 the Georgetown University Pan-American Students' Association was formed.

The School established exchange scholarships for Latin American and other foreign students which, remarked the Washington *Star* in 1930, "are in line with the general policy of the School of Foreign Service to advance the cause of international peace through international understanding.

56. Pope Paul VI sending message of greeting via Telstar to Georgetown University, September 26, 1963, inaugurating the 175th anniversary celebration. On the left, Cardinal Cicognani, Secretary of State; Archbishop O'Boyle on the right.
Pontificia Fotografia Felici

57. How the scene looked to students and faculty on the giant screen set up in McDonough Gymnasium.

58. A colorful moment in the Pan American folklore fiesta honoring Our Lady of Guadalupe.
Photo by Peter Carter

59. Miss Suzushi Hanayagi, one of the great geishas of Japan, in Gaston Hall.
Asia Society, Inc. Performing Arts Program. Photo by Isamu Kawai.

60. Songs in many tongues were heard in Gaston Hall at Christmas, 1963, as Georgetown language students sang carols.

61. Father Gerard J. Campbell, executive vice-president, presenting the anniversary Medal of Honor to Seán Lemass, Prime Minister of Eire.

Georgetown University News Service. Photo by Bob Young, Jr.

62. Barbara Ward speaking at Georgetown on March 20, 1964, on the unity of mankind.

63. Gunnar Myrdal, who had flown in from Stockholm to keynote the anniversary conference on Poverty-in-Plenty, and Leon Keyserling listen to the discussion that followed Myrdal's address on January 23, 1964.

Photo by Peter Carter

64. Luncheon on November 22, 1963, on the site of Old South, honoring Dr. Alberto Lleras Camargo (third from left), former President of Colombia, who was to lecture that evening. A few minutes after this picture was taken, Edward Martin (far left), Assistant Secretary of State for Latin American Affairs, was called to the telephone and then returned to announce the news of the assassination of President Kennedy.
Photo by Peter Carter

65. Within minutes of confirmation of the news of President Kennedy's assassination, Mass was offered on the porch of Old North as students assembled in the yard.
Georgetown University News Service. Photo by Bob Carter, Jr.

66. Chief Justice Earl Warren at the first convocation of the anniversary year, giving the address honoring the memory of his predecessor, Chief Justice Edward Douglass White, of the class of 1863.
Georgetown University News Service. Photo by Bob Young, Jr.

67. Lyndon B. Johnson, then Vice-President, addressing the alumni banquet on October 12, 1963, at the Waldorf-Astoria, New York. Johnson briefly attended Georgetown Law School early in his career.
Georgetown University News Service. Photo by Bob Young, Jr.

68. French philosopher Gabriel Marcel lecturing on "Science and Wisdom."

69. A session of the School of Foreign Service anniversary conference "America and the World: Change and Challenge."
Photo by Peter Carter

70. Reporters at the press table gathering material for their stories on the Poverty-in-Plenty conference.
Photo by Peter Carter

71. "As one who has spent a great deal of time attending similar conferences throughout the United States, I would say that this one was just about tops," wrote Monsignor George G. Higgins of the Poverty-in-Plenty conference in his syndicated column.
Photo by Peter Carter

72. Selassie I, Emperor of Ethiopia, receiving an honorary degree. *Georgetown University News Service. Photo by Bob Young, Jr.*

73. A Georgetown student from Indo-China admiring French products at an exhibit on French Language Day. *Photo by Peter Carter*

74. Pablo Casals plays for the Glee Club at his home in Puerto Rico. *Photo by Thomas Zoss*

75. Professor Laure▯ Leite of George Washing▯ University speaking on ▯ ruary 13, 1964, in Gas▯ Hall on "Naturalism ▯ Contemplation in Baro▯ Painting and Sculpture."▯
Photo by Peter Carter

76. Father Edward B. Bunn, president of Georgetown, celebrating a Solemn Mass at the ceremonies opening the 175th anniversary observance.

. . . The FIDAC, representing the organized war veterans of ten nations, selected Georgetown University as one of five great American institutions worthy of special commendation for their work in the advancement of friendly foreign relations."

Europe was not neglected by the Foreign Service School's students. In 1923 a group visited Poland, and in 1927 and 1928 trips were made to other countries on the Continent.

A special feature of the school's activity throughout the 1920s was its maintenance of a lecture series open to the public. Father Walsh believed that a university owed an obligation to the local community and that this was one means of fulfilling the duty. The value of this service was recognized by the Washington *Post* in the fall of 1928:

Many Washingtonians are taking advantage of the opportunity afforded them this year by the Georgetown School of Foreign Service through its series of public addresses, to hear the views of leading European authorities on educational and political affairs who are visiting in this country. . . . This series of addresses . . . was arranged . . . not only for the benefit of the Foreign Service students but for the general public as well. With few exceptions, their addresses at Georgetown will afford the only opportunity of Washingtonians to hear their views while visiting in the Capital.

ALUMNI AROUND THE WORLD

School of Foreign Service graduates were soon scattered throughout the world in various governmental and private corporation posts. "From Soviet Russia to China," reports a newspaper dispatch of the late twenties in the University archives, "from central Europe to India and South America, students of the Foreign Service School are doing their share in promoting the best interests of the American government." Georgetown men were consuls or consular assistants at Tampico, Valparaiso, Bucharest, Warsaw, Naples, Singapore, and Brussels. Other graduates were serving with governmental agencies or private firms in various portions of the globe. Many became teachers of Foreign Service subjects in schools and colleges in various parts of the United States.

FACULTY ACHIEVEMENTS

Two successive American Secretaries of State requested the professional services of Dr. Leon Dostert, and in 1929 another of the school's experts was drafted "to undertake the revision of the entire financial, commercial, and tariff system of China, at the request of the Chinese government."

Publications by the faculty included *Spanish Origin of*

International Law (1928) by James Brown Scott, *American Foreign Trade,* co-authored by Professor Notz, and numerous other books and technical articles.

No description of the Georgetown University School of Foreign Service would be complete without an account of the contribution made by Father Walsh in his yearly series of public lectures.

From the early 1920s, when he headed the Papal Relief Mission to Russia, he had been convinced of the peril presented to the United States by communism. He would later, in an interview with President Franklin Roosevelt, warn of the peril of trusting the word of any Soviet Russian diplomat. Throughout the twenties and thirties he lectured on communism in Washington and many other sections of the country. He was in particular demand by the American armed forces. One of his addresses to a group of army officers deeply impressed a colonel who would later succeed Harry S. Truman as President of the United States.

An announcement of an early lecture series describes their purpose:

The authorities of the School of Foreign Service of Georgetown University consider the problem presented by Russia as one of the major international issues of the hour. For that reason, and in pursuance of its policy of public service, the School has arranged a series of public lectures on the general topic, "Russia in Revolution." These lectures . . . are designed to sketch the historical background indispensable for a right understanding of the tremendous upheaval in the social, the economic and the political order introduced by the Revolution of 1917 and proclaimed by the Bolshevists as the only basis for the reconstruction of human society elsewhere. The course will moreover furnish material for a dispassionate evaluation of the claims of Soviet Russia to be admitted into the family of nations on the basis of absolute equality.

DIPLOMACY IN PRACTICE

A hint of the school's reputation in 1931 was provided by a query sent to the president of the University by a Chicago *Tribune* reporter: "Is it a fact that an ambassador, appointed by the President of the United States, must select his secretary from Georgetown University . . . ?" Father W. Coleman Nevils, the president, replied, "It is not a fact that any ambassador is ever required to select his secretary from Georgetown University—even though his wisdom in not doing so might be questioned."

Although the Foreign Service School students were not always rewarded in the style imagined by the *Tribune*, they were displaying diplomatic finesse even in small matters. They selected Valerie, the pretty daughter of Austrian Ambassador Prochnik, as sponsor of their ball at the Mayflower Hotel on February 15, 1935.

MORE BUILDING

The 1920s and 1930s were a period of steady expansion of Georgetown's physical plant. Another dormitory, "New North," of 145-room capacity, was completed in 1925. The Old North structure was considerably renovated, a new wing added to the hospital, and work begun on the new medical-dental building on the upper campus. Still another dormitory, "Copley," with de luxe furnishings, was ready in 1929; and shortly afterward the White-Gravenor administration, classroom, and laboratory building was placed in service.

This elaborate construction program coincided with some of the darkest years of the depression era. In February 1933 Father Nevils called this fact to the attention of President Herbert Hoover:

Recently I called a meeting of the directors of Georgetown University to ascertain how we might best cooperate in relieving even in our limited way the present world-wide unemployment situation. . . . In order that we may put in circulation what funds we have and thus extend the credit value of every dollar, our decision is to start at once [the construction of the White-Gravenor building]. . . . We shall be able to keep employed an average of three hundred and ninety-five men for the next nine or ten months. I have taken the liberty of sending this letter as a pledge of Georgetown's confidence and to assure you of our one hundred percent confidence in the efforts of your administration to meet the present national emergency.

With the additional space provided by this structure, the School of Foreign Service classes were moved in 1932 to the upper campus from their temporary quarters at the Law School. All University divisions save that of the Law School were now assembled at or near the Hilltop.

ECLIPSE EXPEDITIONS

The new director of the astronomy department, Father Paul McNally, won international repute for his expedition in 1932 to Freyeburg, Maine, to observe the eclipse of the sun. One photograph made by the Georgetown astronomers was acclaimed as the best picture of total occultation and solar corona secured by any of the observing parties. Father Mc-Nally was besieged with requests from all over the world for prints and slides of this picture. The Yerkes Observatory astronomers pronounced it the best coronal photograph and the richest in detail since the famous one taken by Edward Emerson Barnard and George W. Ritchie on May 28, 1900. The president of the International Astronomical Union, Professor Frank Schlesinger of Yale, expressed his congratulations. The American Association for the Advancement of Science at its 1932 national meeting exhibited a four-by-three-foot unretouched enlargement of the picture.

Other black-and-white plates showed a wealth of detail in both the inner and the outer corona. Clearly marked were the long equatorial wings of light extending for upward of a million and a half miles.

Father McNally was a member of the Georgetown University-National Geographic Society expedition that studied the solar eclipse of 1936 from Kustanani, Russia, and of the expedition sent in the same year by the Society and the United States Naval Observatory to Canton Island in the Pacific to observe the eclipse. He was with the group sponsored by the Society and the United States Bureau of Standards to observe the total eclipse in Brazil on October 1, 1940.

ATHLETICS

Since 1910, Georgetown's football teams had often been rated among the outstanding ones of the East. Some great names had adorned what a historian of sport has called her "rambunctious" elevens. Harry ("Babe") Connaughton, Jim Mooney, Al Blozis, Jim Castiglia, Augie Lio—to mention only a few—were giants in intercollegiate football competition. (Mooney and Blozis were later killed in action in World War II.) The famous game in 1940 between Georgetown and Boston College, lost by Georgetown by a 19–18 score, was declared by Grantland Rice to have been the greatest he had ever watched. In track and field sports, also, the Blue and Gray had been among the leaders, with special glory being garnered by her relay teams.

Georgetown made a difficult decision in 1951. She withdrew from competition in intercollegiate football. The reasons for the move were frankly financial. Expenditures on athletics, it was concluded, were not as important as increases in faculty salaries, the construction of new buildings, and the satisfaction of other academic needs. A disappointed alumni were asked to approve this sacrifice in the cause of academic excellence.

MEN OF MEDICINE

Each June in the troubled years between the two world wars, Georgetown conferred her medical and law degrees on young men who would apply to their professions the University's high ideal of personal responsibility. As Father Walsh repeatedly told his Foreign Service students, what the nation needed was men of character as well as of knowledge.

The fledgling graduates of the former department could look for inspiration to Georgetown's great doctors, past and present—George Kober, Ernest Laplace, Bailey Ashford, George Tully Vaughan, and many others. Kober's achievements in surgery and public health activities had been lauded by the eminent Dr. William Welch himself. "Few men in the medical profession," noted a newspaper at his death in 1931, "have been more prominently identified with the promotion of public health . . . throughout the country." He was credited with being the first to point out the role of the fly in the transmission of typhoid fever.

Dr. Ashford had merited world recognition for his work in tropical medicine in Puerto Rico. He was the first to discover the hookworm in the New World. As a result of his findings the Rockefeller Foundation later started anti-hookworm campaigns in cooperation with other countries. Dr. Laplace, a pupil of Pasteur, Lister, and Koch, was an international name in surgery. Dr. Tully Vaughan had a well-established American reputation in the same field. The standard history of medicine had been written by an alumnus of the school—Dr. Fielding H. Garrison. The book still remains the best in the field.

MEN OF LAW

The School of Law could point to such illustrious alumni as Federal Judges E. Barrett Prettyman and David A. Pine; Charles Fahy, in 1933 First Assistant Solicitor of the Department of the Interior; Frank Hogan, sometime president of the American Bar Association; Leo A. Rover, United States district attorney for the District of Columbia at his retirement in 1934; Michael Igoe, judge of the United States district court of the Northern District of Illinois; Judge Paul Stoner Lusk of the Oregon Supreme Court.

In 1931 Father Francis Lucey took charge of the Law School as Regent. Before the end of the decade he had made three major reforms: (1) a college-degree requirement for admission; (2) a prohibition against a "second try" for students who had failed a major examination; (3) a prohibition against accepting students who had failed at other law colleges. Father Lucey introduced graduate courses in 1938. He also laid the foundations for the present Law Center by acquiring additional contiguous properties for the school's future expansion.

George Hamilton, in two separate terms, served the school as part-time dean for almost half a century. From 1911 to 1943 he had as assistant dean one of the most beloved members of the lay faculty, Hugh Fegan. Fegan's relationship to the students was virtually that of father to son, and his appointment as dean in 1943 was a popular one. He held this post until 1954. Mr. Fegan was a true legal scholar, as well as a man of broad humanistic culture.

THE WALSH LECTURES

The years from 1928 through 1941 saw the rise of nazism and fascism, the development of Russian communism, and the major dislocation of the free enterprise system of the Western World. The period opened with the most disastrous economic depression the United States had ever suffered and ended with the most terrible armed struggle the nation had ever been forced to fight.

During this crucial time, Georgetown University in her

lecture halls reaffirmed day in and day out the truths of the American Declaration of Independence, the American Constitution, the American Way of Life, and the Christian truths of law, freedom, and the inviolable dignity of man.

Georgetown's insistence on perennial truths was most effectively dramatized by the continuing public lectures and writings of Father Edmund A. Walsh. Throughout the thirties he defended American principles and exposed the fallacies of all totalitarianisms, communist or fascist.

The theme of the Walsh lectures of 1935, for example, was "The Progress of Revolutionary Thought: A Study of Social Reform by Evolution or Violence"; at Des Moines, Iowa, in the same year, it was "The Challenge of Communism," a topic he spoke on repeatedly to a crowded Constitution Hall in Washington. In 1939 he gave a public lecture course entitled "The Government and the People of the United States." Earlier he had urged the necessity of fighting communism by social reforms at home. Edmund A. Walsh, in these critical years, was the voice of Georgetown University.

After December 7, 1941, Georgetown University went "all out" to support the nation's war effort. By the end of March 1943, more than half of the thirteen hundred students in the College and in the School of Foreign Service were in the armed forces, and the remaining campus population was steadily decreasing. In less than a month, however, the tide turned with the coming of the Army Specialized Training Program, until the halls of Georgetown soon had more than twice the number of residents they had ever accommodated in peacetime.

Georgetown was one of the institutions singled out by the government for the implementation of an important preliminary phase of the ASTP—the testing and classifying of soldiers previously chosen in the camps of the Third Service Command as potentially eligible for the ASTP. This basic program was called Specialized Training and Reassignment, or STAR. Four thousand, six hundred and eighty-two soldiers spent an average of seven or eight days at the Hilltop, three thousand nine hundred and twenty-eight of whom were allotted—on the basis of tests administered by the Georgetown faculty—to more than fifty colleges and universities throughout the country.

At the beginning of 1944 more than thirteen hundred ASTP students were boarding on the campus. Georgetown, as the large poster proclaimed at the main entrance, was now a military reservation, with armed sentries patrolling the grounds.

The war was the occasion for the breaking of a 154-year-old Georgetown precedent. In the fall of 1944, for the first time, women were admitted as students to a department of the University. The Graduate School led the way. In the early 1960s all of Georgetown's schools were coeducational except the College.

POSTWAR DEVELOPMENT

On July 31, 1947, a new 407-bed Georgetown University Hospital, built on Reservoir Road next to the Medical School at a cost of more than three and a half million dollars, received its first patients. The opening of the hospital marked the beginning of a new era in the history of the University's medical program. In 1949 a team of inspectors of the Association of American Colleges reported:

The Georgetown Medical College has made tremendous strides in improving the quality of its teaching since the last survey in 1939. Great credit should be given the administrative officers who have seen what had to be done and have taken the necessary steps to bring the changes about. The past ten years have been a period of marked progress in most of our medical schools. There are few who have moved more rapidly than has Georgetown.

More specific was a communication from Dr. Francis J. Braceland, of the Mayo Clinic (and at the time a consultant to the Georgetown University Psychiatric Department). "On a visit a short while ago to Georgetown," he wrote in September 1948, "I was delighted to see the forward steps which had been taken since the advent of the new dean, Father McNally. First, and most important of all, he has surrounded himself with an excellent staff. It must have been at considerable investment, for they are all first-class men. The idea of having full-time men in the major branches is an extremely important step and one which I am sure all medical schools will eventually come to. . . ."

Georgetown was now requiring her medical students to take their National Board Examinations at the end of their second and fourth years. This, said Dr. Braceland, is "one of the most forward steps that I have heard about in any medical school in the country."

MEDICAL RESEARCH

From the mid-1940s onward, Georgetown's medical men were engaging in important research. The report of 1949 noted many investigations in progress in the physiology and pathology departments; for example, arthritis and cancer studies, and the problem of radioactive isotopes in calcium metabolism. The hospital soon initiated research work in epilepsy and muscular dystrophy.

In a summary prepared in January 1954, the Medical School dean listed more than thirty research projects then being pursued. Six years later, medical dean Hugh H. Hussey, M.D., took thirty-five typed pages to summarize the research projects under way.

HUFNAGEL'S WORK

Some of the more spectacular original work being done at the Georgetown Medical Center involved the new techniques developed by Dr. Charles A. Hufnagel for the surgical correction of diseases of the heart and blood vessels. From the studies by Dr. Hufnagel and his assistants, there has evolved, according to Dr. Hussey, "a series of major advances in the treatment of hardening of the arteries and congenital defects of arteries."

Original investigations by Dr. Hufnagel led also to the invention of a plastic prosthesis (tube) for insertion into the aorta to counteract the effects of aortic valve leakage. The first application of this method was made at the Georgetown University Hospital in 1952.

On September 11 of that year Dr. Hufnagel operated on a young woman who, because of a badly damaged rheumatic heart, had been given about twelve months to live. This is how the Georgetown surgeon used his new technique:

[He] made an incision in the side and back of [the patient's] chest and exposed the aorta, a grayish-white, pulsating tube. He clamped off the blood flow and removed a small section of the vessel. . . . From several artificial valves of different sizes, Dr. Hufnagel selected the smallest, and gently inserted it into the artery in such a way that it connected the two cut ends. Then over each end he closed a nylon plastic ring to hold the walls of the artery to the valve cylinder. He tied the rings and slowly removed the clamps. People in the operating room now heard a steady click-click-click-click. As the blood coursed through the aorta, it pushed the ball away from the end of the little tube. Click! The ball came to rest in the middle and the blood flowed around it and out the other end. Then the blood pushed the other way. Click! The ball rolled back and shut off the end of the valve on the heart side, where there was no passageway around it. Click! It rolled back and let blood from the heart come through. Click! The valve closed. Click! It opened. And so on. . . . [The patient] was out of the hospital within a month.

By the end of 1956 Dr. Hufnagel had put new valves into about two hundred patients. Further improvements in technique have made it possible to replace parts or all of an aortic valve in cases where it has been destroyed by disease.

Other basic studies have concerned methods for maintaining circulation in the body after arresting the heartbeat (open-heart surgery), methods for restoring the function of the heart after the heartbeat has been stopped for some time in the course of cardiac surgery, invention of specialized mechanical equipment that can function safely as a replacement for the heart during time of heart surgery, and study of methods for suspending animation for significant periods of time (thirty to forty-five minutes) by lowering the body temperature to a point just above freezing.

Dr. Hufnagel has also succeeded in using plastic buttons to patch up broken walls inside dogs' hearts. This research with animals is directed toward eventual surgical repair of one of the most common heart defects in human beings, imperfect partitions of the heart.

The success of transplants of blood vessels has led to an extensive study of the overall problem of transplantation of tissues. Thus, within the Division of Medicine and Surgery there is now a separate laboratory for this purpose, which includes tissue culture and organ culture. Synthetic or mechanical replacements for whole organs or parts of organs are being developed. For example, preliminary studies suggest the feasibility of a new type of mechanical pump to serve as an artificial heart.

THE ARTIFICIAL KIDNEY

Georgetown has pioneered in the use of the artificial kidney for accidental and suicidal poisonings, and has consistently been among the three most active artificial kidney centers in the United States. This device has been described as "a mechanical filter that takes over renal function during uremic poisoning, cardiovascular crises and other acute emergencies associated with kidney shut-down." A dramatic proof of the substitute kidney's efficiency was provided by the case of a young woman treated at Georgetown Hospital in 1951 after she had accidentally swallowed a lethal dose of poison. Both kidneys had ceased to function, and after nine days poisons had accumulated in her system to an extent that her heart was affected. One end of a rubber tube being attached to an artery, and the other end to the machine, the patient's blood was filtered continuously for five hours through one hundred and twenty feet of cellophane tubing wrapped around an electrically-driven drum. The cellophane performed the function of normal kidneys by filtering out the poisons in the patient's blood. After fifteen days the woman's kidneys began to operate.

On another occasion the artificial kidney kept a boy alive during eighty-nine days of kidney failure. In 1955 it saved a forty-four-year-old man who had swallowed the contents of seven bottles of aspirin. This was claimed to be the first successful treatment for an overdose of aspirin already in the bloodstream. The artificial kidney was demonstrated by Georgetown doctors on a national television program on October 10, 1955.

THE HUMAN BRAIN

A joint research program of the Georgetown Medical School and Washington's Doctors' Hospital was engaged in 1951 with the problem of a so-called "misbehavior center" of the human brain. The target for investigation was the front lower edge of the temporal lobe, the part of the brain just behind the ear on both sides. Malfunctioning of, or damage to, this section of the brain had a relationship with the neurological disturbance know as psychoepilepsy. The Georgetown-Doctors' Hospital team was obtaining remarkable curative results by cutting out parts of the gray matter in the critical area.

The Georgetown doctors have never forgotten that a Medical College has a twofold obligation. As expressed in the catalogue:

It is the philosophy of the Department of Medicine that an active research program is essential for modern teaching but also that research activity is itself stimulated by teaching and the care of patients. We believe that the proper intellectual development of the student requires that he work in an atmosphere where his teachers are pushing at the boundaries of medical knowledge and that opportunity should be provided for him to join in this activity. For this purpose, electives are provided to give each student the opportunity to work with one of the medical sub-specialties and thus witness, or even assist, the broadening of medical knowledge. On the other hand every effort is made to project the social aspects of medicine and to help the student visualize the patient in the broad sense. We hold no brief with any jousting between the art and the science of medicine; they are inseparable and complementary.

The dynamism and flexibility of the Georgetown Medical Center's teaching is exemplified in these paragraphs from the catalogue of 1960–1961:

During the academic year 1957–1958, extensive revisions of the medical curriculum were completed. The main objective . . . was to formulate a curriculum geared to advances in medicine without increasing the time required to obtain the M.D. degree. These efforts show an emphasis on fundamental principles, close correlation of basic and clinical sciences, and the avoidance of duplication and overlap of subject matter.

Techniques of teaching have been carefully reviewed and are undergoing continuous evaluation. The panel conference method has been widely adopted in the current program. The format and conduct of each panel is left primarily to the appointed moderator's discretion. (Further research re teaching techniques is in progress.) All curriculum revisions are constantly monitored and reevaluated. The structure of the curriculum permits considerable flexibility. Further changes will be made, based on the experiences gained by these newer courses and methods.

THE LAW CENTER

The postwar story of the legal department of Georgetown is the story of the steady growth of the Law Center, as the Law School now was named. Under the fostering hands of Father Lucey and the faculty he had assembled around him, this important part of the University entered on its finest hours.

The recent catalogue defines the aims of the Georgetown legal educators:

More than a professional school, the Law Center is also a department of a university dedicated to the preservation, transmission, and perfection of the Christian and American cultural heritage. In this heritage, nothing is of greater significance to the civil community than the rule of law. The Law Center, therefore, is committed not only to the formal education of lawyers, but to the understanding, discussion and development of the law itself. This commitment expresses itself through sponsorship of institutional and individual research and writing in the law; through faculty service on public commissions and faculty participation in learned and professional societies; and through presentations to the general public of discussions on the social adequacy of jural norms, the effectiveness of our institutions of justice, and the possibility of alternative legal solutions for the problems of our society.

An important innovation that won for Georgetown another "first" was the establishment at the center in 1960 of the Legal Internship Program. This new training service, open only to recent graduates of law schools, combined expert instruction in the art of trial advocacy in the Graduate School of Law and the actual representation of indigent clients in the courts of the District of Columbia.

High praise for the venture came from President John F. Kennedy in a telegram of July 23, 1962:

It is with pleasure that I extend my warm congratulations to the Georgetown University Law Center upon the completion of its second successful year of the legal internship program.

Professor Shadoan and Associate Dean Pye are to be congratulated for their supervision of the interns in this vital activity. The interns themselves deserve the gratitude of all of us for their competent and courageous representation of those unable to afford counsel. This work is in the highest tradition of the profession. I am informed that the judicial conference for the District of Columbia circuit has recently commended the interns for their excellent performance in this important area. It is gratifying to know that their outstanding work has been so well received.

The legal internship concept signifies the progressiveness of our system of legal education and the activities of your young attorneys represent a significant contribution to the cause of evenhanded justice for rich and poor alike.

Somewhat similar to this project, but essentially differing from it, was the Continuing Legal Education Institute, founded at the Law Center in 1952. The catalogue states the chief purposes of this significant addition to the curriculum:

First, because of the continuing and ever varying developments in the field of general law, the bar and legal educators now recognize that lawyers must now . . . be kept abreast of these doctrinal changes. Secondly, the Institute is teaching what the lawyer calls "practical skills," such as "Trial Tactics and Strategy" and the "Trial of a Negligence Case." These courses in practical skills are not available in the crowded curriculums of undergraduate law schools. . . . Third, since the practice of law is breaking up into specialties the Institute offers the practicing lawyer an opportunity to acquire this specialized knowledge.

The Georgetown teachers of law recognize, as the catalogue explains, "that the Graduate School of a Law Center is the laboratory, the forum, and the cultural center of legal education and research where the student, the scholar, the educator, the lawyer, and the judge may aid in formulating programs that will assist in bettering the administration of justice."

To carry out this plan, the Center has established several research fellowships. Fellows work on research projects that will provide information and aid to management and labor, to the courts, to the government, and the public alike. Most important of these fellowships are those given by the German industrialist, Mr. Schulte Zur Hausen.

"In the field of international law," says the catalogue, the Georgetown University Law Center "is pioneering in the field of International Trade Regulation, offering six related courses in this relatively unexplored field of legal education."

THE INSTITUTE OF LANGUAGES AND LINGUISTICS

The Washington *Times Herald* announced on October 6, 1949:

Georgetown University . . . will score a first in world education when the new institute of languages and linguistics opens October 17.

Father Edmund Walsh was quoted as follows:

It [the new institute] is the natural evolution of the school of foreign service, founded in 1919 in the wake of a great war. Again, in the wake of another great war, it is necessary to train individuals to use languages as links and not as barriers between peoples.

The school, said Father Walsh, was a "venturesome educational experiment" which would adapt technological advances to improve language teaching—"an essential to peace."

These ideas of the founder were further developed in the

new school's first official announcement. The three decades that had elapsed since 1919 had brought to the nation enormously enlarged responsibilities. But a grave defect still remained in our national equipment. It has been charged that Americans are among the worst linguists in the world. It would be the aim of Georgetown's Institute of Languages and Linguistics to remedy this lack and thus "contribute to greater efficiency in meeting our increased international obligations."

The institute's 1963 catalogue calls attention to a broader purpose:

The curriculum of the Institute, at first glance, appears to have a heavy concentration in languages. In reality, the curriculum is one of language study crowned by civilization and literature. The language courses as such, include much of the cultural and behavioral patterns of the country studied. The purpose of this program is to equip students with the language competence and scholarly training necessary to meet the increasing needs at home and abroad for full understanding and easy communication among peoples.

Quartered on Massachusetts Avenue near Du Pont Circle, but later moved to the campus, the institute, from its beginnings, adopted the most modern and original methods of language instruction. This is not surprising in view of the fact that the school's first director was Dr. Leon Dostert. He had been, during the war, interpreter to General Eisenhower and General Giraud, had set up the first simultaneous translation system at the Nuremberg trials, and had later introduced it to the United Nations meetings.

The standard ways of teaching languages were radically readapted. Use was made of technical devices such as recorded material, audio-visual instruments, training laboratories, and individual booths where students might practice what they had learned and repeat what they had heard from the living voice of the teachers.

Special training was provided for interpreting at international conferences, for expert translating and for the specialized positions in international organizations where knowledge of foreign tongues is a prime necessity. To afford training under conditions which duplicate the actual working environment of an international conference, a large multilingual conference chamber was provided. This room was equipped with interpreters' booths, microphones, headpieces, and other facilities similar to those used for simultaneous interpretation at the United Nations.

In a typical course, the student would see no textbooks during the first two or three months. Instead, he would be taught by movies and picture slides and tape recordings representing objects, incidents, and ideas to be interpreted into the language being studied. By means of the multilingual translation instruments, five or more languages can be taught in the same room.

RESEARCH PROJECTS

The institute is now engaged in several advanced research projects. Of these, one of the most significant is the Arabic Research Program, supported by the United States Office of Education. The work of this project is to produce a series of basic courses, reference grammars, and bilingual dictionaries in the cultivated spoken forms of Moroccan, Syrian, and Iraqian Arabic.

The Georgetown English Language Program (GELP) aims at the formation of Turkish teachers of English, for the training of Turkish technicians requiring a knowledge of English to pursue their professional studies in the United States, and for teaching illiterates in the Turkish Armed Forces. The project is in Ankara, Turkey, and has a staff of seventy-five persons.

The Machine Translation Research involves the conversion of Russian into English, and of Chinese into English, by computer. The conversion of Russian into French on the basis of the Georgetown program is in progress, in association with EURATOM in Brussels and Ispra, Italy. The project includes preliminary studies for Chinese-to-English and English-to-Turkish machine translation programs.

A special project under the sponsorship of the Department of Health, Education, and Welfare was initiated in 1961 to train blind students in a form of simultaneous translation. This involves aural reception of recorded materials and typewritten translation into English. In the fall of 1962 a second phase of the program was begun, with thirty trainees in German and Russian and a staff of four instructors. Dr. Dostert pointed out that the need for translators and transcribers, particularly of Russian, is increasing rapidly. Blind students, he believes, offer an untapped source of ability. Indeed, the blind are often better students, he declared, since they are so undistracted in their concentration on auditory techniques.

THE SCHOOL OF BUSINESS

Another offshoot of the School of Foreign Service is the School of Business Administration, established in 1955. Since 1936 the former department had maintained a course in business administration, but not until the later date was the program embodied in an independent division of the University.

If one were to seek the outstanding fact in the history of the School of Foreign Service itself since the end of World War II, it would be this: flexibility joined to firm adherence to the school's original aims. The content and orientation of courses were altered to meet changing circumstances, but the basic purposes were the same. Details of teaching methods were modernized and new courses added, but the fundamental pedagogical strategy remained fixed. The school was aware of her twofold duty in a new kind of world: she must engage herself with contemporary problems while drawing sustenance from her old sound roots.

THE GRADUATE SCHOOL

Georgetown's Graduate School of Arts and Sciences can, in a sense, claim a birth date as early as 1820, since, in the year following the College granted her first M.A. degree. It would be too much to expect a graduate school in the nineteenth century to meet twentieth-century requirements, and after the turn of the century the graduate school developed considerably. Many fine scholar-teachers contributed their talents. Between 1900 and 1940 more than four hundred degrees were awarded. In the early 1940s the school was vigorously reorganized by Dean J. Hunter Guthrie, S.J., in accord with the highest scholarly standards.

Besides numerous articles in scholarly journals, more than 120 books were published by Georgetown's M.A. or Ph.D. students during the decade beginning in 1953. More than 150 books were published during the same period by the school's professors. These figures do not include publications by professors or students of the Medical and Law Centers.

The Graduate School sponsors special extracurricular activities, of which the most important are the Institute of

World Polity, the International Relations Inquiry, and the Graduate Economics Roundtable.

The institute is an enterprise of university scholars throughout the country in association with other specialists in public affairs. It has concentrated its research on the legal and ethical problems raised by modern international conflict, with emphasis upon the revival of the international law of war, regulation of nuclear warfare, and the problems of military occupation. It has published *Prisoners of War* (1948), *Yearbook of World Polity, Studies in International Law and Organization*, Vol. I (1957) and Vol. II (1960).

The Roundtable is a significant part of the program of the Department of Economics. It meets monthly for an evening's work and has a double purpose—personal contact with theoretical and practicing economists, and development of dialectical skill in debate and group work. Many eminent economists have taken part in these meetings.

The International Relations Inquiry is an activity of the Department of Government. It offers annually a series of public lectures by leading experts on international affairs.

THE SUMMER SESSION

An important feature of Georgetown's educational program in recent years has been the Summer Session. Besides the more conventional offerings, this annual academic period includes several topflight conferences and institutes in the areas of contemporary science, literary criticism, philosophical and social thought, and other fields. A Writers Conference has brought to the campus outstanding professional practitioners of fiction. Interdisciplinary studies have been inaugurated in three fields (economics, government, and history) to acquaint students and professional people with basic information on African, Latin-American, and Russian areas. Ancillary to liberal arts studies has been the demonstration of new techniques for the teaching of Latin. Also, since 1962, Georgetown University has directed five Peace Corps training programs and sent overseas as volunteers more than five hundred persons for service in Ethiopia, Afghanistan, Turkey, and Iran.

PLANS FOR GROWTH

Underlying the advances of all the departments in the most recent period of Georgetown's history was a master plan for the University's across-the-board development.

In February 1949 Father J. Hunter Guthrie, S.J., became Georgetown's president. At his inaugural ceremony the basic aims of the University were reaffirmed. One of the most impressive statements of purpose was made by guest speaker Sir Hugh Scott Taylor, Dean of the Graduate School of Princeton University:

Somewhere, somehow he [the scientist of today] dimly apprehends that *scientia* or knowledge must become *sapientia* or wisdom. There are those who sense that the physical and natural sciences require a complementary science which can be found in theology or religion; they sense that this can only be achieved if the material in man can in some way fuse with the Divine. This University is dedicated to an educational process which attempts this fusion of the material with the spiritual, which attempts, in this troubled century, to recapture that unity of life which loves science and its curiosity concerning created things without forgetting that man is the masterpiece of a Creator.

The more specific means required for realizing these high aims were described by the next president of Georgetown, Father Edward B. Bunn, in 1953:

With education and scientific research on the march, Georgetown today can ill afford to continue along the even tenor of her way. She must forge ahead if she is to add new luster to her escutcheon and prove worthy of her mission. To accomplish this, she must become an even finer Georgetown. She needs a broadening of opportunity for her students and an improvement of facilities and tools for her faculty.

Through the years, buildings not only depreciate but often become inadequate or obsolete. The field of man's quest for knowledge is ever broadening and requires the addition of new academic courses or the modification of existing ones. Scientific research and discoveries are not only opening up horizons for the student but are requiring new laboratories and equipment. Professors' salaries have not kept pace with increased living costs. Student tuition has been increased somewhat but has not kept pace with increased costs; endowments have become less productive. These are some of the urgent problems that stand in the way of a finer Georgetown.

To solve these problems, the president announced, a Greater Georgetown Fund was to be established. This was designed to provide opportunities for supporting Georgetown by means of two devices—an "Annual Giving" program and a long-range plan for capital donations and grants. (Since 1945, Father Bunn reported, $8,500,000 had been devoted to the University expansion.)

Like his predecessor, Father Bunn did not forget fundamental postulates. "Unless," he said, "you can do the best possible job, unless you can do a high type of thing, it is not worthwhile trying. It is not worth a man's life to produce something mediocre."

A GREATER GEORGETOWN

How well the aspirations of 1953 were translated into reality can now be seen. During the decade following the inauguration of the Greater Georgetown plan, the University executed her most ambitious development program for any comparable period of time. The achievement involved the physical plant, but also, as Father Bunn had urged, the enlarging and bettering of the quality of professors and student body, the expanding of curriculum, the broadening of research, the increase of student aid and professors' salaries.

Six new buildings were erected—the School of Nursing, the Kober-Cogan Dormitory, the Gorman Diagnostic Clinic, the new School of Foreign Service, the new south dormitory and cafeteria, and the new science building. Moreover, extensive repairs and renovations were made on existing structures. In terms of cost, $15,872,000 was expended on new buildings, and $5,430,597 on building renovation, equipment, and utilities, totaling $21,302,597.

By 1963 the number of teachers was about ten times that of 1900, while the size of the student body was nearly 7000 as compared with 503 in the last year of the nineteenth century. In the fiscal year 1894–1895 the total receipts of the University had been less than $130,000. In 1963 she was capitalized at something more than $50,000,000 and her annual operating expenses were about one-fifth that sum.

Georgetown University had come a long way from her modest beginnings. Early on the morning of September 26, 1963, her faculty and students gathered in McDonough Gymnasium. In silence they watched and listened as Pope Paul VI, whose image was projected from a giant screen, telecast via Telstar a message of greeting and a special blessing to the faculty, students, alumni, and friends of the "Alma Mater of Catholic colleges in the United States." It was an auspicious beginning for the observance of the 175th anniversary of the institution.

It is often difficult to pinpoint the exact moment from which to date the beginning of a school. One could date Georgetown from the year 1788, when construction began on Old South, or from the entry of her first student in 1791. Georgetown has chosen to date her anniversaries from the deeding of the original property to her founder, John Carroll, in 1789, after construction had already begun. By this reckoning she was 175 years old on January 23, 1964. But nearly two centuries of history cannot be properly commemorated in a day, and it was planned to celebrate Georgetown's 175 years with a program of impressive academic, artistic, and social events. Having begun with the history-making telecast by the Pope, it would end on December 3, 1964, the 149th anniversary of the death of Archbishop John Carroll, with a convocation at which the principal address was to be delivered by President Kennedy.

Then came November 22, 1963. It was almost one hundred years since the house diary had recorded in horrified accents the murder of another President, shot through the back of the head while seated at the side of his wife. Now it was John Fitzgerald Kennedy.

The University, like the nation and the world, was numbed with grief. A 175th anniversary lecture by Dr. Alberto Lleras Camargo, former President of Colombia, scheduled for the evening of November 22 was canceled. Other anniversary events set for the following week were dropped.

The University pulled herself together again and faced the future with a strength nourished by her memories of the past. The mourning period over, the program of commemorative events was resumed, bringing world-renowned artists, scientists, educators, poets, scholars, philosophers, theologians, statesmen, and ecclesiastics to the Georgetown campus. The concluding convocation was replanned as a memorial to the fallen President. Lyndon B. Johnson, who as Vice-President had been the speaker at one of the opening events of the anniversary year, quickly and graciously agreed to deliver, as President, the address which John Fitzgerald Kennedy was to have given.

For Georgetown University the year 1964 was a time to look back over 175 years of service to God, to country, and to the world—and forward with confidence and dedication to the tasks of the future.

PRESIDENTS OF GEORGETOWN

Name	*Years*
1. Rev. Robert Plunkett	Oct. 1, 1791–93
2. Rev. Robert Molyneux, S.J.*	June 14, 1793–96
3. Most Rev. Louis Guillaume Valentin Dubourg, S.S. Bishop of Louisiana & Archbishop of Besançon	Oct. 1, 1796–98
4. Most Rev. Leonard Neale, S.J. Second Bishop of Baltimore	Dec. 24, 1798–1806
5. Rev. Robert Molyneux, S.J.*	Oct. 1, 1806–8
6. Rev. Francis Neale, S.J.* acting President	Dec. 9, 1808–9
7. Rev. William Matthews (Alumnus)	Mar. 2–Nov. 1, 1809
8. Rev. Francis Neale, S.J.*	Nov. 1, 1809–12
9. Rev. John A. Grassi, S.J.	Aug. 11, 1812–17
10. Most Rev. Benedict J. Fenwick* (Alumnus) First Bishop of Boston	June 28–Sept. 11, 1817
11. Rev. Anthony Kohlmann, S.J.	Sept. 11, 1817–20
12. Rev. Enoch Fenwick, S.J.	Aug. 2, 1820–22
13. Most Rev. Benedict J. Fenwick* (Alumnus)	Sept. 15, 1822–25
14. Rev. Stephen L. Dubuisson, S.J. (Alumnus)	Sept. 9, 1825–26
15. Rev. William Feiner, S.J.	May 4, 1826–29
16. Rev. John W. Beschter, S.J.	Mar. 31–Sept. 13, 1829
17. Rev. Thomas F. Mulledy, S.J.* (Alumnus)	Sept. 14, 1829–37

* Twice President.

18. Rev. William McSherry, S.J.
    (Alumnus)   Feb. 2, 1838–40
19. Rev. Joseph A. Lopez, S.J.   Jan. 1–Apr. 30, 1840
20. Rev. James Ryder, S.J.*
    (Alumnus)   May 1, 1840–45
21. Rev. Samuel Mulledy, S.J.
    (Alumnus)   Jan. 10–Sept. 6, 1845
22. Rev. Thomas F. Mulledy,
    S.J.* (Alumnus)   Sept. 6, 1845–48
23. Rev. James Ryder, S.J.*
    (Alumnus)   Aug. 7, 1848–51
24. Rev. Charles H. Stonestreet,
    S.J. (Alumnus)   Aug. 1, 1851–52
25. Rev. Bernard A. Maguire,
    S.J.* (Alumnus)
    acting President   Aug. 10–Jan. 25, 1853
    President   Jan. 25, 1853–58
26. Rev. John Early, S.J.*
    (Alumnus)   Oct. 5, 1858–66
27. Rev. Bernard A. Maguire,
    S.J.* (Alumnus)   June 1, 1866–70
28. Rev. John Early, S.J.*
    (Alumnus)   July 14, 1870–73
29. Rev. Patrick F. Healy, S.J.
    acting President   May 22, 1873–74
    President   July 31, 1874–82
30. Rev. James A. Doonan, S.J.
    (Alumnus) acting President   Feb. 17–Aug. 17, 1882
    President   Aug. 17, 1882–88
31. Rev. J. Havens Richards, S.J.   Aug. 15, 1888–98
32. Rev. John D. Whitney, S.J.   July 3, 1898–1901
33. Rev. Jerome Daugherty, S.J.   July 11, 1901–5
34. Rev. David H. Buel, S.J.
    acting President   Aug. 5, 1905–7
    President   Jan. 5, 1907–8
35. Rev. Joseph J. Himmel, S.J.   Aug. 27, 1908–12
36. Rev. Alphonsus J. Donlon,
    S.J. (Alumnus)   Jan. 23, 1912–18

* Twice President.

37. Rev. John B. Creeden, S.J.   May 1, 1918–24
38. Rev. Charles W. Lyons, S.J.   Oct. 5, 1924–28
39. Rev. W. Coleman Nevils, S.J.   Aug. 25, 1928–35
40. Rev. Arthur A. O'Leary, S.J.   July 2, 1935–42
41. Rev. Lawrence C. Gorman,
      S.J.   Dec. 17, 1942–49
42. Rev. J. Hunter Guthrie, S.J.   Feb. 17, 1949–52
43. Rev. Edward B. Bunn, S.J.   Oct. 10, 1952–

ALMA MATER

Sons of Georgetown, Alma Mater,
Swift Potomac's lovely daughter,
Ever watching by the water,
    Smiles on us today.

Now her children gather 'round her
Lo, with garlands they have crowned her,
Reverent hands and fond enwound her
    With the Blue and Gray.

Chorus

Wave her colors ever,
Furl her standard never,
    But raise it high,
    And proudly cry,
"We're Georgetown's sons forever!"

Where Potomac's tide is streaming,
From her spires and steeples beaming,
See the grand old banner gleaming—
    Georgetown's Blue and Gray.